– COACH –

Daniel Stewart

*with "Be Mindful"
contributions
from Vanessa Roman*

BOLDER, BRAVER, BRIGHTER

The Rider's Guide to Living
Your Best Life on Horseback

TRAFALGAR SQUARE
North Pomfret, Vermont

First published in 2021 by
Trafalgar Square Books
North Pomfret, Vermont 05053

Disclaimer of Liability
The author and publisher shall have neither liability nor responsibility to any person or entity with respect to any loss or damage caused or alleged to be caused directly or indirectly by the information contained in this book. While the book is as accurate as the author can make it, there may be errors, omissions, and inaccuracies.

Trafalgar Square Books encourages the use of approved safety helmets in all equestrian sports and activities.

Library of Congress Cataloging-in-Publication Data
Names: Stewart, Daniel, author.
Title: Braver, bolder, brighter : the rider's guide to living your best
   life on horseback / Daniel Stewart.
Description: North Pomfret, Vermont : Trafalgar Square Books, 2021. |
   Includes index. | Summary: "Coach Daniel Stewart, author of the hit
   mind-and-body equestrian workout Fit and Focused in 52, is back with new
   plans to power you up, bolster your confidence, and supply you with the
   mental tools you need to be all you can be, in and out of the saddle.
   With Coach Stewart's infectious optimism and indomitable sense of fun,
   readers will find themselves embracing exhilarating changes in their
   outlook and their abilities"-- Provided by publisher.
Identifiers: LCCN 2020045526 (print) | LCCN 2020045527 (ebook) | ISBN
   9781646010325 (paperback) | ISBN 9781646010332 (epub)
Subjects: LCSH: Horsemanship--Guidebooks.
Classification: LCC SF309.254 .S74 2021 (print) | LCC SF309.254 (ebook) |
   DDC 798.2--dc23
LC record available at https://lccn.loc.gov/2020045526
LC ebook record available at https://lccn.loc.gov/2020045527

All images used under license from Shutterstock.com *except:* p. 3 (by Megan Beyer at Altitude Equine Photography; pp. 7, 8, 27, 44, 47, 54, 86, 92, 96, 114, 120, 124, 140, 188, 191, 192 (right), 258, 268, 272 (by Shannon Brinkman Photography)

Fergus the Horse cartoons by Jean Abernethy and used with permission

Book design by *Katarzyna Misiukanis–Celińska*
Cover design by *RM Didier*
Index by *Andrea M. Jones (www.jonesliteraryservices.com)*
Typefaces: *Minion Pro, Metropolis, Blacksword,* and *Zooja Pro*

Printed in China

10 9 8 7 6 5 4 3 2 1

– dedication –

*To my daughter Emma,
son Luca, and wife Severine.*

*Our lives are changing so fast,
but the one thing that will never change
is my love for you.*

*You will never know
how proud I am
to be your father and husband.*

V

PART TWO: *Braver* 121

INTROD

THE SECRET TO HAVING IT ALL IS KNOWING THAT YOU ALREADY DO.

UCTION

I've coached thousands of equestrians in my life, and even though all of them were unique and special in their own unique and special way, I've always asked the exact same thing of them: "Be kind to yourself and others, do your best, be okay when your best isn't enough, and finish what you start." Perhaps not surprisingly, these are also the same things I've always asked of my wife, children, myself, and everyone else that I've ever believed in.

We're all like fingerprints, unique and special in so many different ways, but we all share the same dream of living a life that feels bold, brave, and bright. Whether you define yourself as rider, athlete, student, or teacher, you're in control of your own definition. You, and only you, can define how you'll treat yourself and others; how you'll act and react in the face of fears, frustrations, and failures; and whether you'll struggle or shine after mistakes, mess-ups, and missed opportunities.

So, how do you define yourself? Do you define yourself as a victim or a survivor? Do you define talent as something that's fixed or something that can grow? Do you define yourself by the mistakes you make or by the effort you made? Do you compare your body and behaviors to others, or believe that being the best (or better than the rest) is the only ruler by which to measure success? Do you define yourself as a failure simply because you failed? In the end, everything that means anything to you simply comes down to how you define yourself. *How you treat you.*

You really only get one shot at this, and by this, I mean *life*. It's my hope that *Bolder, Braver, Brighter* will help shine a little light on the many surprising and empowering things you can do to create a life that feels powerful, mindful, and hopeful, instead of powerless, mindless, and hopeless—a life that's defined by feeling worthy and never worthless.

●●● Write Your Own Story

Imagine leaning against a tree while your horse grazes happily beside you. You feel the warm sunshine and breeze on your cheek, hear the chirping of nearby birds, and smell the fragrance of the grass and wildflowers. Your horse nickers quietly and all you can think about is how lucky you are to have this horse and this sport and this life—right here, right now.

Now visualize the same scene, only this time, imagine thinking anxiously about the horse show tomorrow. Imagine worrying about all the people who'll be watching—the judge who'll be judging and the 12-year-old rider who beat you last time. Imagine hoping your horse doesn't refuse the first jump and you don't forget your course like last time. Imagine dreading you'll be the only overweight or underprepared rider there, and that you'll mess up and let down everyone who's counting on you.

Wow! That kind of ruined the story, didn't it?

The second story contains the exact same horse, tree, and field; the only thing that changes is the story built around it. But that's all it really is. Just a story, a piece of fiction made up by worrying about what might happen in the future or wishing something hadn't happened in the past. But it changes everything. It removes the joy, pleasure, and happiness from the story. It changes a feel-good novel with a happy ending (or romantic comedy depending on your horse!) into a horror story with a dreadful ending. Even though they're just silly stories, it's pretty clear they're going to have very different endings.

So, what story and which ending are you going to write? I hope my book helps you write a story about self-belief, self-esteem, and self-confidence. A story about how you never quit, made excuses, compared yourself to others, or shied away from challenges. A story about how you overcome fears and failures, remain positive in negative situations, and hold it together when it would be normal to fall apart. This is the kind of story that's inside you.

No one's perfect (nope, not you either), but only you can write your story. Judges, spectators, teammates, trainers, and family members might appear in your story. Failures, fears, mistakes, and mess-ups will definitely appear in it. Riders who are more experienced, stronger, taller, thinner, and better than you will also be in there, but it's up to you  to decide what role they'll play, and what ending you create. Becoming bolder, braver, and brighter doesn't mean you'll never fail or be afraid, it means you'll always have the courage to be the author of your own story.

WIKIPEDIA SAYS:

Status Quo

Derived from the Latin phrase, status quo, which means existing state, and is most often used to describe a resistance to change or progress.

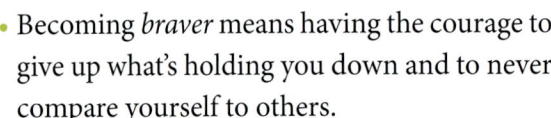

Hard work beats talent, when talent doesn't work hard. ▶

●●● Bolder, Braver, Brighter

Becoming *bolder* means embracing change and challenges. It means developing the desire to do what's hard when it would be easier to do what's easy. It means learning to love yourself and all your weaknesses, fears, and flaws (and all the rest of your bent and broken pieces).

- Becoming *braver* means having the courage to give up what's holding you down and to never compare yourself to others.

- Becoming *brighter* means finding the strength to swap a *why-even-try victim mindset* with a *watch-me-succeed survivor mindset*.

- Becoming bolder, braver, and brighter is hard work, but you're not afraid of a little hard work—after all, you're an equestrian!

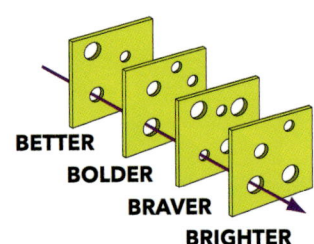

BETTER
BOLDER
BRAVER
BRIGHTER

▲

Becoming the best version of yourself can be as tricky as riding through holes in Swiss cheese. Being bold, brave, and bright is the best way to get through what you're going through!

●

Being bolder, braver, and brighter means embracing efforts and errors and believing that the rewards are always worth that effort. Being *bolder* requires you to step outside your comfort zone and accept being vulnerable as you fail your way to success. Being *braver* requires you to be patient and delay immediate gratification in exchange for achieving long-term goals. Being *brighter* requires a desire to try and accept new things at a time when old things seem acceptable. Being bolder, braver, and brighter is tough, but so are you!

Behaving bolder, braver, and brighter means rejoicing change and rejecting status quo, never choosing to do the same thing over and over again because you know you're capable of more. *Bold* riders know they're not supposed to *go* through life, they're supposed to *grow* through life. *Brave* riders know that growth doesn't happen when they always think like they've always thought or act like they've always acted. *Bright* riders know that if they always do what they've always done, they only get what they've always gotten. Behaving bolder, braver, and brighter means knowing that to get something you've never had, you're going to have to do something you've never done.

●● The Monkey and the Coconut

Hunters have developed a surprising way to capture monkeys. They drill a small hole in a coconut, pour out the milk, and replace it with

succulent fruit. They then re-hang the innocent looking coconut back in the tree and wait for a monkey to come along. When a monkey arrives and notices the fruit, it forms its hand into a point, slides it inside the coconut, and grasps the fruit. But, when it does, its previously thin hand becomes a fist too large to pass back through the small opening. And then he's stuck—stuck up in a tree with no escape because his hand is too large to exit the hole. Unless, of course, he decides to release the fruit. Which he doesn't. So now all the hunter has to do is walk up to the coconut and place the monkey into a sack. No more monkey.

So what does this story have to do with becoming bolder, braver, and brighter? Well, perhaps it's a metaphor reminding you to never hold onto things that can hurt you—to become mindful of what they are and to just let go of them.

So what are you holding onto that can hurt you? What should you let go? Is it worrying about judges or comparing yourself to others? Is it fear of letting someone down or fear of messing up? What's your fruit? Take a few minutes and have an honest conversation with yourself, knowing that if you can just let go of what hurts you, you'll no longer be held captive by it. Perhaps becoming bolder, braver, and brighter simply comes down to reminding yourself to never be a monkey—and to let go of things that can hurt you. ●

1

GOOD, BETTER,
BEST. NEVER REST
UNTIL YOUR GOOD
IS BETTER, AND
YOUR BETTER
IS YOUR BEST.

bolder

bolder

One day you're going to do everything right and it'll still go wrong. You'll give 100 percent and still come up short. You'll do your best, but your best won't be good enough.

This statement might sound a bit defeating but it's neither negative nor pessimistic. It's simply a fact. It's not because you're not good enough or talented enough or smart enough. It's because success doesn't mean you're always going to succeed, being a winner doesn't mean you'll always win, and doing your best doesn't mean you'll always be the best or better than the rest. Sometime, you'll do everything right and it'll still go wrong.

You can't go through life without picking up a few emotional bumps and bruises. Life's made up of a series of mistakes and milestones, struggles and successes. It's only human to fall down, mess up, and be afraid from time to time. Frustration and failure are in your future and they're just as important as your successes. You just need to be *bold* enough to believe it.

●●● Kintsugi

When something breaks you throw it away. After all, it's no longer perfect. But there's a 400-year-old Japanese tradition called *Kintsugi* that might provide you with another alternative.

Kintsugi is the art of putting broken pieces of pottery back together by filling their cracks with gold. Instead of hiding the imperfections, they embrace, accentuate, and celebrate them as part of the object's history. By repairing the broken pieces, they create brilliant scars that make the object more unique and valuable than before. Those who practice *Kintsugi* believe the scars should be shown off and admired because they give the object even greater strength and beauty.

This same philosophy can be used for embracing your imperfections. Instead of trying

to hide your broken pieces, embrace your flaws, and believe that you don't have to be perfect to be perfect. Teach yourself that your fears and failures—while a part of your history—can combine together to form the gold that

WIKIPEDIA SAYS:

Bold

The quality of possessing self-belief and courage while freely engaging in unfamiliar and challenging situations without hesitation, doubt, or fear.

▲

Did you know? When a broken bone has healed, it becomes stronger than it was before the break. Struggles and stress create strength!

Of course
you're
cracked.
How else
will all your
brightness
come out!

makes you stronger. Everyone is damaged in some way, but when you're bold enough to embrace your broken pieces, you'll become more valuable than ever before.

●●● Wondering, Wishing, and Worrying

In any other context, these words might seem completely innocent, and in fact, *wondering* and *wishing* are even quite positive, but when *doubt, dread,* and *defeat* enter the picture, they quickly go from harmless to harmful. For example, "I *wonder* what the judge is thinking; I *wish* I was as good as her; and I *worry* about letting my trainer down." Or, "I *wonder* why everyone is better than me; I *wish* I wasn't so short; and I *worry* about making a mistake." *Wondering, wishing,* and *worrying* can get you into a lot of trouble. *Bold, brave,* and *bright* riders know it and avoid it. This book is about overcoming wondering, wishing, and worrying. ●

DON'T LET YOUR ICE CREAM MELT
WHILE YOU'RE WISHING YOU HAD
SOMEONE ELSE'S SPRINKLES.

1

chapter

be an original,
not a copy

1

chapter

When your horse makes a mistake, do you love him less? When you see a bigger, fancier, or more talented horse, do you love him less? When he's nervous loading or afraid of the scary butterfly in the corner, do you love him any less? If you're like most, the answer is always *no*.

But when you make a mistake, do you love yourself less? When you see a taller, thinner, more talented rider, do you love yourself less? When you're nervous of failing or afraid of the judge, do you love yourself any less? Unfortunately, if you're like most, the answer is usually *yes*. Maybe all you need to do to become bolder, braver, and brighter is just to treat yourself like you've always treated your horse....

You're an original. There's no one else quite like you. No one acts or reacts quite like you, shares your hopes and dreams, or wonders, wishes, and worries as you do. You're

Be the role model you needed when you were younger. ▶

an original, and originals are always more valuable than copies.

This chapter is about *you*. It's *not* about how you compare to others or how you think others see you. It's just about you. It's about how you fall and get back up, celebrate and love yourself. It's *not* about anyone but you, because only you can achieve these things. No one compares to you and that's the real value of you. Being bold comes from being proud of who you are and embracing all the brave and bright pieces that make you unique.

I'm going to start this chapter with a promise. A promise that one thing can change everything. A promise that when you just remove one thing from your life, every second of every minute of every hour of every day will feel bolder, braver, and brighter. A promise that if you just remove one thing, you can remove all the wondering, wishing, and worrying.

Yikes! That's a pretty bold statement. Saying one thing can change everything. That one thing can remove most of your fears, frustrations, and freak-outs! But it's true, and you'll agree after reading the next few paragraphs. That one thing is called "out-grouping."

*be*LIEVE IN *you*RSELF

●●● Out-Grouping

Out-grouping is wondering, wishing, and worrying about other people. It's about worrying what they think of you and how you think you compare to them. It's about trying to live up to the expectation of some people, while worrying about letting others down. It's about comparing yourself to others and feeling bad because they've achieved more or failed less than you. It's about thinking of the judge when you should be thinking about your first jump, and worrying about the crowd when you should be thinking about your last one. It's about spending all your time trying to be like one person while trying not to be beaten by another. It's about feeling certain you'll do poorly because everyone else is doing so well, and feeling uncertain you'll do well because everyone thinks so poorly of you. It's about worrying that your performance won't make your trainer happy, or nervous it'll make your teammates sad. It's about feeling as if you're a failure just because you failed, and about wishing you looked more like someone else—and less like yourself.

Out-grouping is bad. Out-grouping is about comparison and wondering, wishing, and worrying. You *wonder* what other people are thinking about you, you *wish* you were as good as them, and you *worry* you never will be. Out-grouping leads to body envy, shame, perfectionism, defense mechanisms, and a fear of failure. The constant *compare and despair* caused by out-grouping leads to low self-confidence and even lower self-esteem. Out-grouping is the one thing that changes everything. Get rid of it, and you get rid of wondering, wishing, and worrying. Get rid of it, and you become bolder, braver, and brighter.

Out-grouping isn't about you. It's about everyone else but you, but it robs *you* of everything you desire and de-

Don't let what's on the outside get in. Ships only sink because water gets inside them. Out-grouping is like water. It's only when you let it in that it can hurt you. Focus on your inner strength rather than comparing yourself to those around you. When you keep out-grouping from getting inside, you keep it from sinking your ship!

serve. Happiness, joy, contentment, gratification, achievement, success, self-respect, pride, peace, and pleasure all exit when out-grouping enters; it's completely worthless because you have no control over the thoughts and behaviors of anyone but yourself.

Get rid of out-grouping and you get rid of fears, frustration, and freaking-out. Get rid of it and you become bolder, braver, and brighter. This chapter is about the promise that one thing can change everything. This chapter is about out-grouping.

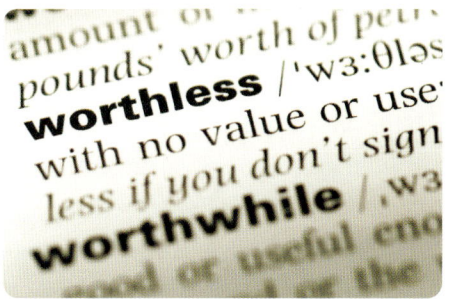

▲

You are not worthless, or worth less than anyone else. You're an original, and originals are always valuable!

●

●● Body Envy

There's a good chance you've experienced body envy. It's the feeling of

10 COMMON EXAMPLES OF OUT-GROUPING

1. Worrying about what the judge is thinking. ●

2. Feeling nervous riding in front of a crowd. ●

3. Hoping an opponent will do poorly. ●

4. Wishing you looked like someone else. ●

5. Trying to live up to the expectations of others. ●

6. Hoping you won't let someone down. ●

7. Feeling like others have progressed faster than you. ●

8. Wishing you were as good as someone else. ●

9. Worrying about what others think of you. ●

10. Comparing yourself to others. ●

THEM AND YOU

Judges judge you, competitors compete against you, and spectators watch you. There's no shortage of them in our sport. Your job is to do what you can do to learn, and what you can to improve. The next time you worry about them, simply tell them that you will do your best. This changes your focus from them (and what they're thinking), back to you (and what you can do). Even if your best isn't good enough, both them and you will know that you have given 100 percent and that's all them and you could ever ask for.

self-dissatisfaction when you compare yourself to someone who appears taller, skinnier, prettier, or more *Instagram perfect* than you. It's the feeling of inadequacy when you measure yourself against someone who has longer legs or has taken a short-

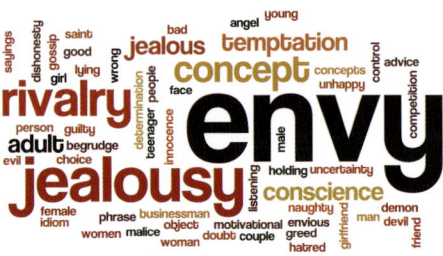

er time to get where you've gotten. These thoughts might only last a moment, but their impact can last a lifetime because they can replace your pride with pressure. The *pride* you feel in yourself is replaced with the *pressure* to be like someone else. But it's not an even trade: you're getting the short end of the stick because pride beats pressure any day—and after all, past a certain age, your legs just aren't going to get any longer!

In addition to *body* envy, you might have also experienced two other forms of envy: *talent* and *possession* envy. *Talent* envy is like body envy, only instead of comparing your physical *traits* to others, you compare your physical *abilities* to them (like their winning percentage or how they make everything look easy). *Possession* envy occurs when you compare your possessions (like horse or trailer) to those of others. Together I like to call these three forms of envy: traits, talents, and toys.

Envy isn't the same as greed or jealousy. Greed is the desire to have more of something, but envy is the desire to have something possessed by someone else. Jealousy usually involves three people and creates distrust and a fear

STOP ENVY

of loss (like when a boy is afraid his girlfriend might like another guy). Envy, on the other hand, creates feelings of inferiority and shame (about not being good enough) and only involves two people: the person you are, and the person you wish you were.

Shame

Shame always accompanies envy. You've always been told (especially by me!) to believe and take pride in yourself, so it's understandable that feeling envious might also make you feel a bit disappointed in yourself. This lays the foundation for shame—not only wishing you had the traits, talents, and toys of someone else, but feeling bad about feeling those things.

Envy and shame are two of the most hurtful forms of out-grouping. Few things in this world are more heart-breaking than feeling *less than*—feeling as if you're not good enough, attractive enough, or talented enough, or being embarrassed to be you because you don't feel you

STOP SHAME

measure up to others. This is why envy is one of the seven deadly sins. It holds you back from becoming the best version of yourself because it makes you believe you like someone else's version better.

Why try and fit in when you were born to stand out?

Shame is often confused with guilt, but they're not the same thing. Shame always focuses on a person (you), but guilt focuses on a behavior or action. As a result, shame makes you see yourself as a bad person, but guilt only makes you feel like a good person who did a bad thing. When you experience shame, you say things like, "I am bad," but when you feel guilt, you only say, "I did something bad." The difference might seem small, but shame is much more hurtful than guilt because the pain it creates comes from disapproving of who you are, rather than what you did.

●● Causes of Body Envy and Shame

Comparing yourself to others, being dissatisfied with yourself, wishing you were like someone else, and wanting what others have are four signs of envy and shame. But why do you feel them in the first place? Here are the four reasons:

● You Learned It

Being envious started a long time ago. As a child, you went through a phase when you wanted all the toys all the time, especially if those toys belonged to someone else! You threw tantrums and cried because you wanted what someone else had (sound familiar?) and just when you

UPWARD AND DOWNWARD SOCIAL COMPARISON

When feeling shame you might try to protect your ego by comparing yourself to someone better, or worse off than you. These are called upward and downward social comparisons. An upward comparison would be protecting your ego after a disappointing ride by telling everyone you were competing against a well-known, high-performance rider. A downward comparison would be receiving time faults on course, but making yourself feel better by comparing yourself to someone who was disqualified. ●

24

started to outgrow childhood envy, you began to feel the same nagging feelings toward your brother or sister. Enter sibling rivalry, which is just envy directed toward a loved one. No wonder envy and shame are so common. You've been practicing them since you were a kid!

● You Saw It

Instagram, Facebook, Snapchat and other social media platforms can cause body envy and shame by:

1. *Creating unrealistic beauty standards (people only sharing their best photos after applying filters to remove their wrinkles and pimples).*

2. *Publishing critical and hurtful messages about someone's appearance ("She's too big for that horse!").*

3. *Linking self-worth to the number of likes, friends, or followers you receive.*

Magazine covers and Hollywood movies are guilty of creating the same unrealistic expectations. No wonder envy and shame are so common. They're on every screen, laptop, tablet, and device you've ever owned!

Learn from the mistakes of others – you can't possibly live long enough to make them all yourself!

25

● You Heard It

Every teacher and trainer you've ever had gave you a 100 percent effort. They did their best 100 percent of the time, but sometimes their 100 percent might not have been enough. Body envy and shame happen when a teacher delivers criticism in a way that feels more belittling and bullying than motivating and mentoring. Criticism is a necessary part of improvement, but when delivered in a way that embarrasses or shames you, the delivery is flawed, not you! No wonder envy and shame are so common. You've been learning it from some of your teachers for a long time.

● You Felt It

You learned it, saw it, and heard it, but there's also a chance you might've felt it at the barn, too. Your barn mates might also (intentionally or unintentionally) contribute to feelings of envy or shame. Gossips and groups (cliques) are a breeding ground for body shaming, so if you've ever felt excluded or picked on at the barn, there's a good chance the seeds of envy and shame might've been planted. Add a little trash

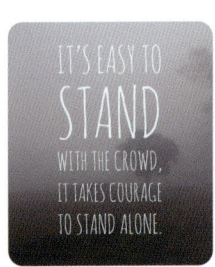

talk from opponents trying to *psych you out* and those seeds might have gotten watered. No wonder envy and shame are so common. You can even find them at the barn!

Be the type of person you'd like to meet.

Be bold or italic,
never regular.

As you can see, body envy and shame are caused by others, but only you can stop them. Learning to love yourself, appreciate what you have, value your strengths, and accept your weaknesses are the keys to stopping them. Learning to define yourself by your efforts rather than your appearance or outcomes is the only way to achieve fulfillment. Perhaps your body shape, equitation, or results are different than others, but you're an original, and originals are valuable!

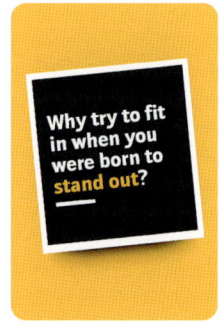

Why try to fit in when you were born to stand out?

Being Belittled or Bullied

You might recall riding for a trainer who tried to teach you to be *tough* by teaching you in a *tough* manner. Instead of reinforcing persistence and rewarding effort, the teaching style might have made you feel more like you were being belittled and bullied. Unfortunately, overly critical teaching methods (*intimidation and humiliation* rather than *motivation*) have been proven to

▲

In Buddhism, the word *Irshya* is defined as being envious and unable to accept the excellence of others. The word *Mudita* is defined as taking joy in the good fortune of others. *Mudita* is therefore the antidote to *Irshya* and the solution to envy and shame.

●

cause riders to feel inadequate, shame, fearful of failure, worried about letting people down, and disappointed in themselves.

While the intention was good (to teach you something), the delivery was bad because your brain always responds the same way when you're feeling attacked (physically or *verbally*). You become tense, tight, and tentative as your brain prepares to flee or freeze. This is why so many riders struggle to perform for threatening coaches, and why many of those riders end up quitting the sport altogether. Verbal threats cause your brain to *freeze* (leading to frustration because you just can't seem

> A good coach can change your position, but a great coach can change your life.

to do anything right), and *flee* (eventually giving up because riding is no longer satisfying, rewarding, or even enjoyable).

The good news is that modern coaching programs are now certifying a new breed of trainer—a coach who's educated using the latest sport-performance and athlete-development data. One who knows that performance only goes up when a rider doesn't shut down. One who doesn't believe toughness comes from being able to hold back tears of shame, or return tomorrow after crying all day today. A coach who realizes that the social and emotional skills learned at the barn are just as important as the physical ones.

But…not everyone gets a trophy!

Modern coaches don't necessarily believe everything is about rainbows and unicorns. They understand the value of failure and mistakes, and help their students experience, accept, and learn from them. These trainers don't give *participation* awards. They know if you're winning every class, you're entered in the wrong

classes. They know if you're not failing or making mistakes, you're just not trying hard enough. But they'd never allow you to take these experiences personally, meaning they'd never allow you to feel like a mistake just because you made one, or feel like a failure because you failed. These trainers aren't necessarily

BODY SHAMING

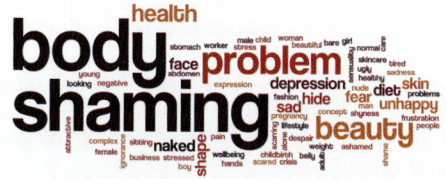

This is making critical or humiliating comments about a person's appearance like, "You don't have the right body for riding," or "You'd be a better rider if you lost weight." Always remember that riding isn't about how much weight you carry, it's about how you carry your weight! Critical or humiliating comments about a person's appearance (such as "You don't have the right body for riding," or "You'd be a better rider if you weren't so fat") have no place in our sport. ●

> Sticks and stones may break your bones, but bullying will break your heart.

always warm and fuzzy (and may even use a stern voice) but they know that being overly cold and prickly will make it nearly impossible for anyone to learn what they've been tasked to teach.

Inappropriate coaching occurs in many ways. Recognizing and becoming mindful of them is an important step to overcoming them. The importance of this cannot be overstated. Below are 10 signs a trainer might be doing more *insulting* than *instructing*:

31

*Never pump yourself up
by putting someone else down...
...Never look down on others
unless you're helping them up.*

- Make insulting remarks about your ability.
- Make shaming comments about your body.
- Verbally abuse you in front of others.
- Compare you negatively to other riders (often in front of them).
- Question your commitment to our sport.
- Humiliate you by teasing, mocking, or making fun of you.
- Constantly remind you of your past mistakes and failures.
- Call you a failure or say that you'll never amount to anything.
- Talk bad about other coaches.
- Insult, gossip, or spread rumors about you, or other riders.

Most coaches who employ these tactics aren't usually aware they're doing it, but unfortunately some are incapable of changing (or even admitting that change is required). Many simply do it because their coaches did it, but it doesn't change the fact that learning can't occur when a student feels threatened or intimidated. The job of a coach is to mentor and motivate. Teaching through intimidation or humiliation is simply using the wrong tools for the right job.

⬤⬤⬤ Why You Do What You Do

A very small percentage of riders make it to the national or international level. This means that the vast majority of equestrians simply ride for the love of the horse, to enjoy the experience, develop physical and social skills, be outdoors and athletic, and enjoy time spent with their friends and teachers. If you feel a coach is standing between you and any of this, remember that you have a choice. You can break the pattern, take back control, and regain your self-esteem by following these four tips:

1. *Remind yourself that coaches are doing their best (even though it's not very good). Perhaps they coach this way because they grew up with a trainer who intimidated or humiliated them. Doing this helps to put you in a position of control, and allows you to stop feeling responsible for their actions. Taking the high road by trying to see the best in the worst teachers, is what'll start you down the road toward regaining your confidence and control.*

2. *Have an honest conversation with the coach. Let him or her know exactly how you feel and be prepared to give examples of when you felt humiliated, insulted, bullied, or belittled. You might even want to prepare a written script and read from it during the meeting (it's so hard to remember things when you're nervous!). This will be difficult, but without the courageous effort, change won't occur (for you or any other rider).*

33

KIDS
AND COACHES

Sometimes it can be difficult to tell the difference between a tough coach and a bullying coach (especially since young riders are taught to respect authority) so here's a good rule to follow. If anyone ever insults you, makes fun of you, or makes you feel ashamed of being you, you can probably assume he or she is a bully. Since the effects of bullying can last from a *long time* to a *lifetime,* stand up for yourself by doing the four things above, and the four things below:

1. Never blame yourself for someone else's bad behavior. ●

2. Tell yourself there's nothing wrong with you, only the way the message was delivered. ●

3. Remind yourself that bullying is never acceptable, regardless of where it happens. ●

4. Tell a parent who only wants the best for you—and you deserve it! ●

3. *If coaches accept the conversation (many won't) offer to help them by scheduling additional meetings so you can offer them periodic updates. This will help them become more mindful of their actions (and become a better coach) while also helping you feel like you're no longer the problem, but a part of the solution.*

> ▲
>
> My son Luca teaching a team-building workshop to a group of equestrians enrolled in my Lake Placid equestrian athlete training camp. The promise of our sport's tomorrow lies in the hands of the promising young teachers of today!

4. *If your coach resists your attempts to help, find a new coach. The time spent with your horse, sport, and riding mates is just too valuable to allow anything (or anyone) to take it away from you. Maybe you'll have to drive a little farther to get to the new barn, but at least you'll be looking forward to getting there!*

Our sport is moving in a very positive *coaching* direction. Many of today's young riders are becoming the coaches of tomorrow and are doing so by participating in certification courses that employ modern sport-performance and athlete-development techniques that differ greatly from the *intimidation and humiliation* coaching styles that were so often taught in the past.

> When perfection
> is driving you, shame
> is riding beside you
> and guilt is that annoying
> backseat driver!
>
> *Brené Brown*

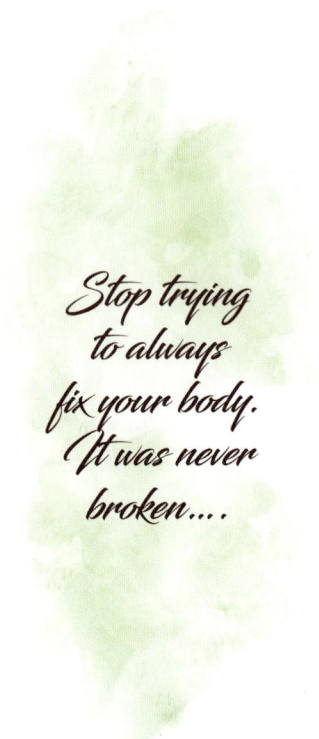

*Stop trying
to always
fix your body.
It was never
broken....*

●●● Fixing Body Envy, Shame, and Bullying

You're wonderful and worthy and deserve to believe it, but it doesn't come from hoping you'll get the traits, talents, and toys of someone else, and it doesn't come from being intimidated or humiliated. It comes from developing a strong *inner* sense of pride, self-respect, and self-satisfaction that says, *I'm enough.* Never try to be like someone else or impress someone else. You're too busy liking yourself.

●●● Self-Schemas and Self-Concept

You have ideas and beliefs about other people. You think your friend is kind, his brother is smart, and his sister is hard-working. Descriptive categories like these are called *schemas.* You also describe yourself using similar schemas, meaning you can also see yourself as kind, smart, and hardworking (or mean, dumb, and lazy). When all your *self-schemas* come together, they form your self-image or *self-concept.* Your vision of you.

Self-schemas begin forming in early childhood based on feedback from friends and family and continue developing throughout life as you meet new people, enter new groups, and experience new things. They're shaped by the roles you play (i.e. rider, competitor, spouse, or parent) and are influenced by your education, appearance, relationships, gender, and age. Successes,

– Valuing You Exercise –

*Learning to love yourself starts with liking and valuing yourself.
Here's a writing exercise that can help you do it:*

☆ **Find strength...** Write two things you do well. Focus on what you do, rather than how you look.

A: ....

B: ....

☆ **Find gratitude...** Write two things you're grateful for. Focus on things you have that make you happy.

A: ....

B: ....

☆ **Find acceptance...** Write two sentences that remind you to accept yourself (such as, "I'm an original not a copy").

A: ....

B: ....

☆ **Find value...** Write two things you like about your body.

A: ....

B: ....

☆ **Find good in others...** Write two things you like about others' imperfections (accepting them helps you accept yourself).

A: ....

B: ....

☆ **Find help...** If body envy, shame, or bullying continue to impact your life, please reach out for help. Here are three websites that can get you started:

www.now.org/now-foundation/love-your-body/
www.centerforchange.com/battling-bodies-understanding-overcoming-negative-body-images/
www.stopbullying.gov

Tell yourself you're good enough for long enough and you'll start to believe it!

failures, and *out-grouping* also play a role. For example, out-grouping will impact your self-concept if you believe everyone is better than you.

The best thing about self-schemas is they influence your behavior, but the worst thing about self-schemas is they influence your behavior! When they create a positive self-concept, you ride with confidence, calmness, and courage, but when they create a negative self-concept, you ride while wondering, wishing, and worrying (tell yourself you're not good enough for long enough, and you might actually start to believe it!). Becoming mindful of your self-schemas, and the impact they have on your self-concept, are what can help you become bolder, braver, and brighter.

●●● Mirroring

You're a mirror, I'm a mirror, everyone's a mirror—but not in the *Who's the fairest of them all* kind of way. Mirroring refers to copying (reflecting) the actions, attitudes, and behaviors of other people. It's like looking into a mirror and acting in a way that reflects what you see there. For example, spend time with kind and

– Self-Concept Exercise –

*Take a few minutes to answer the following three questions.
Don't rush and be as honest as possible. Are you optimistic, kind,
and patient? Hardworking, persistent, and a good teammate?*

☆ **What is your greatest physical strength?**

....

☆ **What is your greatest mental strength?**

....

☆ **What do you admire most about yourself?**

....

Now comes the fun part. Using your self-schemas above, write a complete sentence using the words *proud* and *love* to connect them together. It'll look something like, "I'm a hardworking rider who's *proud* of my ability to never quit, and *love* that I'm respectful of my teammates.

I'M ....
WHO'S PROUD OF ....
AND LOVE THAT I'M ....

This is your *self-concept statement*. It's what makes you unique and valuable and capable. Memorize it, write it, and tape it to the inside of your helmet, tack trunk, trailer, or anywhere else you see often. The next time you want to feel a bit bolder, braver, or brighter, just repeat it to yourself while smiling and taking a few deep breaths. If you believe it, you can achieve it!

confident riders and there's a good chance you'll become kind and confident (you'll begin to reflect what you see in those mirrors). Unfortunately, mirroring can be used for good or evil,

Mirror mirror on the wall,
I'll always get up after I fall,
and whether I walk, trot,
or have to crawl,
I'll set my goals and
achieve them all.

meaning you may also reflect negative actions, attitudes, and behaviors by spending time with negative people. For example, if you want to get good at gossiping, just hang out with people who gossip.

Mirroring is called a *social-contagion* because the actions, attitudes, and behaviors of the people in your social group are contagious. This provides you with a very important choice. You can surround yourself with positive mirrors (and catch a little of what they've got) or surround yourself with negative mirrors (and catch a little of what they've got). The choice is yours, and it's a really important one, so choose wisely!

RUN YOUR OWN RACE

A runner went for a leisurely jog, spotted another runner, and began chasing him down. Before long she caught and passed him, only to realize she'd missed her turn and had to backtrack to get home. Sure she'd caught the other runner, but he didn't even know it was a race! If he did, she might still be chasing him! ●

★ MORAL OF THE STORY:

It's okay to be motivated by others, but always run your own race. Find your own motivation.

41

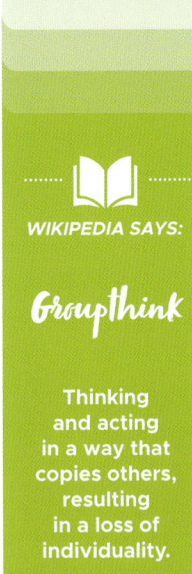

WIKIPEDIA SAYS:

Groupthink

Thinking and acting in a way that copies others, resulting in a loss of individuality.

●● Broken Mirrors

People who display negative actions, attitudes, and behaviors are called *broken mirrors*. Body shaming, blaming, and bullying other riders are all examples of things you can catch from a broken mirror, and just like a real broken mirror, they can really hurt you. So, instead of reflecting what you see in broken mirrors, surround yourself with mirrors who project positivity, self-respect, and self-compassion (those who

The Power of I Am!

Becoming mindful of your actions, attitudes, and behaviors can shift how you feel. Can you connect to the power that helps you stay present and focused on you? Who are you right now, in this moment, and what are you telling yourself? Is it kind and compassionate?

The next time you ride, say these two words to yourself, "I am…"

So, how do you finish the sentence? Are your words encouraging? Are they coming from a place of compassion? Do you feel empowered when you hear them? "I am" and the words that follow can be your strongest tools because they remind you to check in with how you're feeling and what you're focusing on.

Creating an empowering "I am" statement can take you from feeling fearful to fearless, and from crushed to confident. "I am ready, I am capable, and I am excited" can transform any mindless chatter into mindful power. ●

TRUE STORY

A dog tried crossing the road but didn't make it. Sadly, her hind legs were crushed by an oncoming car. Her family rushed her to the vet who said the dog would recover but would never use her hind legs again. She was going to have to pull herself around with her front legs only. The vet then gave the family more news. Their dog was pregnant! Several weeks later she gave birth to a healthy litter of puppies, but the most unusual thing happened when they began to walk. Even though they were healthy, they all learned to walk by pulling themselves with their front legs only!

There's no mystery as to what happened here. The puppies observed their mother and mirrored her behavior. Mirroring of physical and mental traits happen in many animals including monkeys, dolphins, birds, and dogs. ●

love and take pride in themselves) knowing there's a really good chance you'll reflect what you see in them!

In addition to avoiding negative mirrors, remember that you're also a mirror! Your actions, attitudes, and behaviors are also contagious and will be mirrored  by others. So instead of simply avoiding negative mirrors, work hard to become the best version of yourself so that broken mirrors can reflect what they see in you. Self-respect, pride, and gratitude are a few of the many things other people deserve to catch from you. ●

THE BEST VERSION OF YOU
NEVER TRIED QUITTING
AND NEVER QUITS TRYING.

2

chapter

the best version of you

2

chapter

You are the *sum* of your experiences, choices, and actions. When they're *positive* they *add* up to a life that feels *bold, brave,* and *bright.* When they're *negative* they *subtract* joy from your life. Apparently math is more important than you thought! Only this is a new kind of math, one that *adds* meaning to your life instead of *subtracting* happiness from it. Math is power, stay in school!

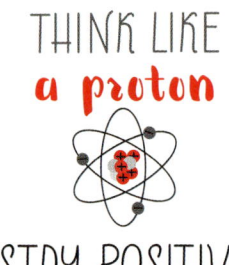

THINK LIKE
a proton

STAY POSITIVE

In order to add meaning to your life, you might need to subtract a few behaviors or habits that can hold you back from becoming your best version. *Wondering, wishing,* and *worrying* are three such habits. Comparing yourself to others, feeling like a failure (just because you failed), and

> Do what you've always done and you'll get what you've always gotten. If you want more, you'll have to do more.

dwelling on mistakes are a few others. The only problem is that change is hard and breaking old habits is even harder! Sometimes it's just much easier to do what you've always done, even though making a few bold and brave changes could lead to a brighter life.

●●● Instinctual Drift

The tendency to avoid *subtracting* bad habits and *adding* good ones is called *instinctual drift*. It's natural for you to

> There's no shortcut to any place worth going.

drift back into old habits because they become like an *instinct*. New Years' resolutions are great examples. Moti-

vated to make a positive change, you make a resolution to exercise more or work less, but that path is long and full of non-motivating twists and turns. That's why 80 percent of all resolutions don't make it past February. People just *drift* back into old habits because habits are *instincts*, and instincts are hard to break!

There are many ways to overcome *instinctual drift*, but all must first begin with a deep desire to really change. Simply wishing to be better, happier, or more successful isn't going to be enough to overcome the drift. You have to really want it. Perhaps it comes from a troubling emotion (called a *mental catalyst*) like crying in the arena for the first time or disappointing yourself for the hundredth time. Regardless of the reason, change is productive and productive is positive, but

BE
mindful

What Do You Choose?

The flow of your day is a result of your choices. How you start your day, end it, and everything in between is a result of the choices you make. Each day you make internal (mental) and external (physical) choices that shape the direction of your daily experiences. Your self-talk is an example of an internal choice that forms your inner voice. Is it compassionate and mindful? The horse you ride and where you ride are examples of external choices that determine how you spend your day. Are they satisfying and fulfilling? Becoming mindful of your choices allows you to understand and adjust them if needed. Take a moment to consider your internal and external choices. Is there something you'd change? Would you like to do anything differently? Can you see a different path?

The power of choice is one of your most valuable tools. You're the creator of these choices, and you have the power to determine how they will shape and transform your experiences.

TRUE STORY

Changes and injuries have one thing in common. Little changes and little injuries seem minor, but can cause major problems! For example, when you break your ankle (big injury), you take care of it right away, but only sprain it (little injury), and you might ignore it for months. Even though the sprain is less, it can hurt you more and for longer. Little changes can make a big difference.

A farmer with a weird sense of humor attempted to teach a pig to put a coin into a piggy bank. In the beginning the pig seemed excited and motivated by the new challenge, pushing the coin around with his nose and then grasping it in his mouth so he could deposit in the piggy bank. Encouraged, the farmer assumed the pig would continue to improve, but before long, the pig lost interest and went back to his old habits of just rooting in the dirt and rolling in the mud. No matter what the farmer tried, no more coins in the piggy bank. ●

★ MORAL OF THE STORY:

Change is hard and breaking old habits can be even harder. The drift to go back toward instinct is just too strong. Especially if there's a pig and a piggy bank involved!

going against your instincts can be difficult, so always make sure you are ready to believe in yourself as much as you believe in the need for change.

●●● Self-Sets

In the last chapter, I taught you that your self-schemas and self-concept work together to create problems or possibilities (p. 36). In this chapter,

49

I'll introduce you to several other self-mindsets (called *self-sets*) that also influence that outcome. The first self-set is *self-awareness,* which is being aware of your emotions, strengths, weaknesses, drives, and goals—and understanding the impact they have on your potential and performance. Here's a list of things associated with strong self-awareness:

1. *You assess situations realistically, optimistically, and with a sense of possibility.*

2. *You're neither overly critical, nor unrealistically hopeful.*

3. *You're aware that your feelings and behaviors can impact your performance and your horse.*

4. *You have the courage to acknowledge a poor performance and take responsibility for it.*

A second self-set that affects your potential and performance is *self-regulation.* This is the ability to control (or eliminate) negative and doubtful thinking, remove judgment, and think before acting. Here's a list of things associated with strong self-regulation:

1. *You cope well with changes and last minute surprises.*

2. *You avoid impulsive reactions and instead focus on finding more appropriate responses.*

Problems only happen when you think without acting or act without thinking.

3. *You have bad moods like everyone else, but never direct anger toward others or your horse.*

4. *When you make a mistake, you're more interested in identifying the cause than a scapegoat.*

When self-awareness and self-regulation come together, they help to create many other positive self-sets. Let's talk about the six most important now.

⊙⊙ { **1** } Self-Respect

Self-respect forms the foundation for how you act, react, and feel about yourself. Having self-respect allows you to accept and appreciate your abilities without constantly evaluating them as good or bad. It allows you to avoid comparing yourself to others, accept responsibility for your actions,

Self-Respect

and fight for your beliefs. Riders with self-respect like themselves regardless of success or failure, and therefore, are less likely to feel envy or shame.

⊙ Boost Your Self-Respect

To respect something is to accept it, so *respecting* yourself means *accepting* yourself. Learn to respect and accept everything about you, including your fears, failures, and flaws. They all offer character-building feedback, so turn them into an advantage by learning how to learn from them. When you accept yourself and respect your efforts, you end up accepting and respecting yourself.

⊙⊙ { **2** } Self-Esteem

Self-esteem refers to how much you appreciate yourself (how much esteem you have for yourself). To esteem someone is to hold him or her in high regard. Self-esteem, therefore, is evaluating and holding in high regard your efforts, behaviors, and emotions (even the negative ones). Self-esteem

Believe in yourself.
No one else will do it for you.

- KOBE BRYANT -
Professional Basketball Player

makes you feel optimistic and motivated, and helps you bounce back from adversity, cope with failure, and avoid feeling shame.

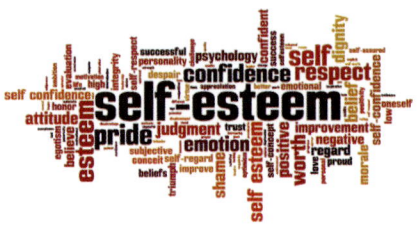

●● Boost Your Self-Esteem

Boost your self-esteem by becoming mindful of the triggers that deflate it. Self-esteem comes from appreciating

yourself and your efforts (instead of your outcomes), so teach yourself to find pride in everything you do (even those things you don't do well). Remember, outcomes are often few and far between, but efforts happen all day, every day. Anyone can appreciate success, but appreciating struggle and setback is a skill. Without it, there can be no self-esteem.

●● { 3 } Self-Worth

Recognizing your worth and finding value in yourself is the foundation of self-worth. Riders with high self-

IMPOSTER SYNDROME

Low self-worth is so common it's been given a name: riders with imposter syndrome attribute their success to luck (not talent or effort), and therefore, usually feel unworthy of praise. They also fear that others will discover they're not as good as they might seem (that is, they'll be exposed as an imposter).

worth have unshakable faith in themselves and don't let it fluctuate with every success or failure. They feel worthy and deserving of good things, even if it doesn't happen immediately. They never compare themselves to others or overly seek the approval of others because they know it would mean placing other people's opinions before their own.

Improving Your Self-Worth

Evaluating your every move in a negative way and comparing yourself to others are two signs your inner value is undervalued (that you feel other riders are more worthy). Improving your self-worth, means investing in yourself. It means, learning to find value in your efforts and experiences regardless of whether they're successful or not. Self-worth doesn't come from finding value in others (wanting to be like them), it comes from investing, and finding value in yourself.

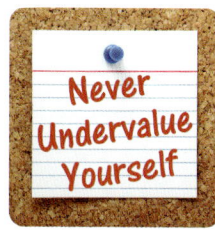

{ 4 } Self-Compassion

Self-compassion means showing kindness to yourself after a disappointing ride, mistake, or failure. Anyone can feel disappointment in such situa-

53

You don't really know what your best is...because your best is yet to come.

tions, but riders with self-compassion remind themselves to appreciate their efforts, regardless of whether they succeed or fail. They know that being imperfect and failing is inevitable, so they're able to rebound quickly, forgive themselves, and avoid being overly self-critical. These riders know it's okay to not always be okay.

Improving Your Self-Compassion

Having compassion for yourself is no different than having compassion for someone else. You notice someone's suffering (for example, a compassionate rider wouldn't ignore a fallen rider), respond with caring and kindness, and then find ways to make the rider more comfortable. The same is true for self-compassion. Notice when you're suffering (for example, feeling envious or afraid), respond with care and kindness, and make yourself more comfortable by removing any self-criticism or judgment.

If you were able to believe in Santa for eight years, you can believe in yourself for five minutes.

55

with an
trips.
char·ac·ter /'kærək
munity, race, etc)
or moral qualities
different from ot
the

> Your character is defined by what you do when you think no one is looking.

●● { 5 } Self-Efficacy

Self-efficacy is the belief that you're capable of coping with challenges and you have the talent required to overcome situations that feel might otherwise feel overwhelming. It's what makes you rise up and make an *effort* instead of give up in defeat. Self-efficacy is The Little Engine That Could ("I think I can, I think I can") combined with Dory from *Finding Nemo* ("Just keep swimming…") and defines how much motivation, optimism, and effort you'll put into a challenge.

● Improving Your Self-Efficacy

Defining your successes by the effort you give rather than the outcome you get, is the key to self-efficacy. Effort means everything to all you do, so teach yourself to rise up to challenges and give up at nothing. Developing the habit of always making an effort regardless of rewards or outcomes will prove that effort and achievement always go together. Without one you can't have the other.

●● { 6 } Self-Actualization

Self-actualization is the *feeling you feel* when completely and entirely self-satisfied, fulfilled, and doing everything in life you'd ever hoped for. It's the *actual-*

ization of your full personal potential. You've left *wondering, wishing,* and *worrying* behind. You no longer compare yourself to others but have self-respect, self-esteem, self-worth, self-compassion, and self-efficacy. You feel enlightened; you've found true meaning and purpose in life!

● Improving Your
   Self-Actualization

Self-actualization is the culmination of all other self-sets. You're free from the envy and shame, you embrace your fears and failures, and naturally direct respect, worth, compassion, and esteem toward yourself. Self-Actualization means you've created the best possible version of yourself, you love yourself, and are 100 percent happy with who you are. Self-Actualization happens when *wondering, wishing,* and *worrying* are replaced with *bolder, braver,* and *brighter.*

If my mind can conceive it, and my heart can believe it, then I can achieve it.

- MUHAMMAD ALI -
Professional Boxer,
Activist,
and
Philanthropist

TRUE STORY

was rushing to begin a workout but couldn't find my earbuds. I always exercise to music so this was a big problem. I looked everywhere: in the kitchen, garage, and between the couch cushions, but no luck. Just as I was about to give up, I found them—they were in my ears all along! ●

★ MORAL OF THE STORY:

Self-actualization is like earbuds. It's been inside you all the time; you just need to remember it.

Impulse control is the ability to control your emotions before they take control of you. It's also the key to avoiding *out-grouping* and achieving self-actualization. You can achieve (or improve) your impulse control by (1) identifying things you have control over, (2) identifying things you can influence, and (3) identifying things you have *no* control or influence over. This is called the *control-influence model* and it helps you to avoid out-grouping and achieving self-actualization because you become aware of what you can (and cannot) control. In doing so, it helps you identify the best ways to direct your efforts.

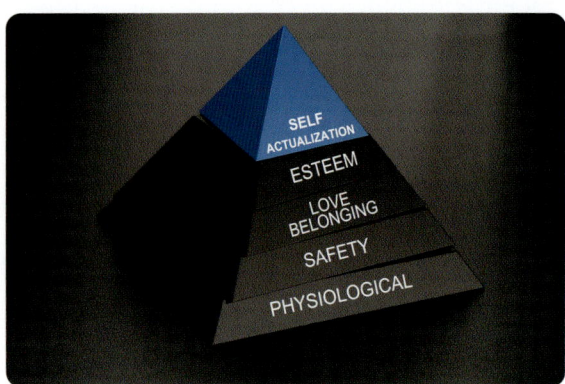

Self-actualization happens when you satisfy all your most important needs. These include: physiological (food and rest), safety (wear a helmet!), love and belonging (feeling like you fit in and are valued), and esteem (self-confidence and self-respect).

(Spoiler alert: it's never toward things you can't control or influence!)

The goal of impulse control is to train your brain to avoid wasting time focusing on things you have no control or influence over. Out-grouping (including body envy and shame) are two such things. Impulse control helps you understand and accept that you can't *control* what the judge is thinking, or *influence* how well your opponents look or ride, but that you can control your decision to respect yourself, learn from your mistakes, and find value in your efforts. Below is a brief list of things you might want to include in your control-influence model:

Identifying what you can control and influence can help you find the best way to direct your efforts.

CONTROL	INFLUENCE	NO CONTROL OR INFLUENCE
Learning from your mistakes	Learning from others	How successful others are
Being a good student	Broken mirrors	What others think of you
Respecting your teammates	Learning new skills	Not letting people down
Showing gratitude	Achieving your goals	How others look or ride
Valuing your efforts	Improving your horse	What the judge is thinking

– Control-Influence Exercise –

*Create your own control-influence model
using the prompts below:*

☆ I can control:

A: ....
....
....
B: ....
....
....

☆ I can influence:

A: ....
....
....
B: ....
....
....

☆ I cannot control or influence:

A: ....
....
....
B: ....
....
....

Should've, Would've, Could've

Out-grouping and *self-actualization* are also influenced by your self-talk, so *impulse control* should also target the words you say to yourself. If you tell yourself you're not good enough for long enough, you'll never eliminate out-grouping or achieve *self-actualization*. Replace them with a little self-respect, esteem, worth, compassion, and efficacy, and everything will change, simply because your self-talk has changed. While you might not have control over everything, no one controls your self-talk but you!

> Never worry about the "could haves." If it "should have," it "would have"….

Tell yourself that you *should* be better than an opponent or that you *should* win, and you're bound to feel a bit disappointed because you have no control or influence over either. Expanding *should* to *should've* only makes it worse. Telling yourself you

GET REAL

There are two people inside you right now (don't worry, it's only a metaphor), and they control whether should and should've will play a role in your riding. Your realistic self is you when you define yourself realistically (strong yet imperfect), set realistic goals (attainable), and hold realistic expectations (successful with a few bumps along the way). Your unrealistic self is who you become when you think in terms of should and should've, because it causes you to define yourself unrealistically (I should be perfect), set unrealistic goals (I should win), and hold unrealistic expectations (success should be easy). Unfortunately, your realistic self knows it's incapable of achieving unrealistic expectations. Can't we all just get along? ●

61

should've beaten an opponent or *should've* won only adds salt to the wound because you're now feeling bad about things you can't control or influence, and that've happened in the past! The word *should* creates speculation about the future and regrets about the past, so the solution is clear. You should stop saying *should*!

●●● **Seven Ways to Improve Your Self-Sets**

Here are seven tips to help you to create your best self-sets, and the best version of yourself:

1. ***Treat others with respect.*** You can't treat yourself with respect if you don't know how to treat others with respect. Make it a way of life by treating everyone, including yourself, with more respect.

2. ***Learn to accept compliments.*** You resist compliments when your self-esteem is low so give it a boost by learning to respond with simple statements like, "Thank you, that means a lot to me."

3. ***Replace self-criticism with self-compassion.*** Instead of judging yourself for mistakes made or opportunities missed, learn to forgive yourself by reminding yourself that your effort was admirable even though the outcome wasn't.

Today you are you, that is truer than true. There is no one alive who is youer than you.

- DR. SEUSS -
Author

4. ***Treat yourself like a friend.*** Most people show more compassion to others than themselves. Next time you struggle, practice a little self-compassion by asking yourself what you'd say to a friend—and then say it to yourself.

5. ***Run your own race.*** Comparing yourself to others causes envy and shame and lowers your self-esteem and self-worth. Learn to boost them by reminding yourself that riding isn't a race, and if it were, you'd be the only one entered.

6. ***Apply for that job.*** Make a list of your strengths and experiences as if describing yourself in a job interview. You might just be surprised at how much good stuff you've forgotten about yourself!

7. ***Love yourself.*** Becoming your best version starts with self-actualization and loving yourself. Accept all your bent and broken pieces that you know you're capable of fixing and straighten them. Always love yourself; you're the only one you've got! ●

CAR MIRRORS ARE SMALL
COMPARED TO WINDSHIELDS
BECAUSE WHAT LIES
BEHIND YOU ISN'T AS IMPORTANT
AS WHAT LIES IN FRONT OF YOU.

3

chapter

watch out for your blind spot

> When limiting beliefs are removed, so are your limits.

3

chapter

Few things will stand between you and success more than you and your thoughts when those thoughts are defeating and doubtful. Negative thoughts are often called *limiting beliefs* because they *limit* how much you *believe* you can achieve or succeed. It's not because you're incapable of success, it's simply because unintended (and unwelcome) thoughts might convince you otherwise. For example, there's little chance you'll ever be able to sit a horse's trot if you continually tell yourself you *can't* sit it. It's not because you're incapable of it, it's because your *belief* has placed a self-imposed *limit* on what you can achieve. Tell yourself that you *can* sit that trot (and work hard to make it happen) and you'll remove

the limit that once stood between you and that trot. In other words, when you remove limiting beliefs, you remove your limits.

I can't cook. I'm not good at math. I'm not a morning person.

I can't sit his trot. I'm not as good as everyone else. I crumble under pressure.

Limiting beliefs are common and it's possible you've even used a few already today. They're the sneaky negative thoughts you don't think you're thinking, even though you're thinking them! The good news is that becoming mindful of them is the key to stopping them. Sometimes, they're just hiding in a kind of *mental blind-spot* and need to be brought out into the light.

The next time you tell yourself you can't do something, do it twice and take pictures!

TRUE STORY

Monkey Experiment

Researchers placed four monkeys in a cage. In the center of the cage was a large tree with a bunch of tasty bananas hanging from the tallest branch. The first monkey climbed the tree but as he reached for a banana, the researchers opened a hidden ceiling door and poured ice water on him! Startled and scared, the monkey scampered down the tree and back to the safety of the group. Almost immediately a second monkey climbed the tree but suffered the same startling surprise. This continued until all four monkeys had attempted to grab the bananas, and had experienced the ice cold water. Now none of them dared to try it again.

But here's the neat part. The researchers removed one of the original monkeys and introduced a new monkey to the group who immediately climbed the tree, but as he did, the three experienced monkeys grabbed onto him so he couldn't continue. In time, he gave up and returned to the group. The researchers then removed another original monkey and introduced a new one to the group who also attempted the climb but gave up after being continually pulled down.

But here's the really neat part: one at a time, the researchers removed all the original monkeys and replaced them with new monkeys until all four had never experienced the ice water before, but none of them would dare climb the tree! They didn't know why, but they didn't even try. They simply believed they couldn't do it. ●

★ MORAL OF THE STORY:

Never let yourself (or anyone else) limit what you believe you're capable of achieving. The next time you think you're incapable of doing something, just go get your bananas!

●●● Blind-Spot Biases

Blind-spot biases are a unique form of limiting belief that lie just below the surface of your awareness (the negative thoughts you don't think you're thinking even though you're thinking them). They're called "blind-spot biases" because, like a car hidden in your blind spot, they pose a threat to you because you're unaware of them. When a car leaves  your blind spot, however, the threat it creates leaves too. Likewise, when negative thoughts leave your mental blind spot (because you become mindful of them) the threat they create also leaves. That's the purpose of this chapter, to introduce you to the many different kinds of blind-spot biases so you can remove them from your mental blind spot.

 There are many different blind-spot biases. I'll introduce you to eight of the most common here. Don't be surprised if some seem a bit familiar, you've probably used a few in the past. Remember, when you can become aware of these hidden negative tendencies (make them leave your mental blind spot) they'll stop bothering you.

●● { 1 } Telescoping Bias

The *telescoping bias* occurs when you view your defeats and disappointments, mistakes and mishaps, and fears and failures as if looking at them through a telescope (so they appear bigger than they actually are), but then view your strengths and successes as if looking at them through the wrong end of the telescope  (so they appear smaller than they actually are). The telescoping bias magnifies your shortcomings and minimizes your strengths and successes. Remember, it's important to be mindful of your shortcomings, but it's also important to see them for their actual size. You can avoid the telescoping bias by teaching yourself to turn the telescope around. Magnify your strengths and successes, and minimize your disappointments and defeats!

●● { 2 } Bandwagon Bias

The *bandwagon bias* is the unintentional habit of believing something to be true, simply because someone said it was so. Without making an effort to fact-check or do due diligence, you simply adopt the opinion of someone because he or she believes it to be true. Worrying about a judge because someone said she's mean, or dreading a jump course because someone said it's scary, are two examples of *jumping on the bandwagon*. The problem hiding in your blind spot isn't the judge or the course, it's believing something to be true without first trying it! You can avoid the bandwagon bias by always fact-checking what you hear. Who knows, maybe that judge isn't so mean or that course isn't so scary—but you'll only know if you give it a try.

I could agree with you but then we'd both be wrong.

COCONUT ATTACK!

Did you know you're twice as likely to be killed by a coconut than a shark? Not only are coconuts more dangerous than sharks, they fall at random (or you fall trying to get them) regardless of whether you provoke them or not! Images of shark attacks, however, are way more vivid (scary) and easy to recall so that's why you spend more time worrying about shark attacks than coconut attacks. ●

●● { **3** } Availability Bias

The *availability bias* (or *heuristic*) happens when you assign greater importance to events that are vivid (scary), recent, and easy to recall. Unfortunately, this can sometimes blur the line between reality and *what just comes to mind* first (what's most *available*). It can also trick your brain into thinking there's an increased likelihood of bad stuff happening again (even though it's not true). For example, remember when you had a bad fall and couldn't stop thinking it might happen again? That was your brain acting on information that was vivid (scary), recent, and easy to recall (even though falling again is no more likely to happen than it was before). You can avoid the availability bias by reminding yourself that thinking bad things might seem natural, but that the possibility of them happening again doesn't increase just because it happened before.

●● { **4** } Self-Serving Bias

Remember the time you received a great grade on a test in school? You were proud of yourself and attributed it to studying hard, paying attention, and doing your homework. Now, remember the time when you did poorly on a test? Only that time, you attributed it to the teacher doing a poor job, test questions that were unfairly confusing, and not having enough time. Perhaps you did the same thing after winning show jumping or losing dressage. As you might have guessed, the *self-serving*

MATH TEST

My son received an 89 percent on a math test recently. He was proud of himself and accepted responsibility for the imperfect score, but was disappointed when the teacher didn't return the test to him. He knew if he could just see his mistakes (move them out of his blind spot) he'd have a better chance of understanding them in the future. Smart people do make mistakes, but it's their mistakes that make them smart! ●

bias arises from a willingness to accept the *fame*, but not the *blame* (it *serves* you well to accept the good, but not the bad). You can avoid the self-serving bias by reminding yourself that it takes courage to take responsibility for all parts of your riding: the good and the bad. Remember, mistakes are your best teachers, but you can't learn from them if you're not willing to pay attention to them.

●● { 5 } Bad-Guy Bias

The *bad-guy bias* happens when you think other people (judges, spectators, competitors, etc.) are thinking bad things about you (criticizing your position, posture, performance, for example). The reason it's called the "bad-guy" bias is because you assume they're thinking *bad things* about you—meaning you assume they're *bad people* (after all, only bad people would think bad things about good people!). But that's the bias part—it's not true! The majority of people are good people just like you (doing their best and enjoying their horses). You can avoid the bad-guy bias by simply reminding yourself that it's unkind to think everyone is unkind, and if people really are thinking bad things about you and hoping you'll do poorly, they're certainly not very deserving of your thoughts.

●● { 6 } Spotlight Bias

The *spotlight bias* is similar to the *bad-guy bias*, only instead of assuming everyone is bad, you overestimate the amount of time you think everyone is watching and noticing you. You just get so used to focusing on yourself that you assume everyone is also focusing on you (when, in fact, they're busy focusing on their own thoughts and struggles). In other words, you feel like you're under a spotlight. Unfortunately, the spotlight bias makes you self-conscious and anxious, which often causes you to avoid attempting difficult tasks because you're afraid something bad might happen (failure) and that everyone will notice. You can avoid the spotlight bias by reminding yourself

BAD T-SHIRT

I n a well-known (and humorous) experiment, a college student was asked to wear a yellow Barry Manilow T-shirt to class. Even though he felt under the spotlight, and told the researchers he was certain everyone noticed (and laughed at) the embarrassing shirt, follow-up interviews found that less than half of the other students even noticed it. ●

FISHBOWL EFFECT

T he feeling you're in a fishbowl where everyone can see what you're doing and criticize your imperfections. ●

that you just might not be as interesting to other people as you are to yourself—and if they do notice you messing up, they probably don't care about it nearly as much as you do!

●● { 7 } Finished-Product Bias

The *finished-product bias* occurs when you compare yourself to a high-performance rider and think things like, "I wish everything came as easily to me as it does to him," or, "She's so lucky to be able to ride so well without having to try." In addition to the obvious problem of comparing

73

yourself to another rider (really bad idea by the way), you also forget that it's hard to make something look easy! It likely took that rider years to make it look that way. The finished-product bias is like comparing apples to

It's okay to be a work in progress. Experts built the Titanic and look how that turned out!

oranges, only instead, you compare a work-in-progress (you) to a finished-product (that rider). You can avoid the finished-product bias by reminding yourself that a *pedestal rider* (the one you put on a pedestal) used to be a work-in-progress, too. There was once a time that rider couldn't canter without ending up on the neck either!

●● { 8 } Confirmation Bias

Confirmation bias occurs when you form an opinion and then alter your thoughts and behaviors so you can make your opinion appear correct (thereby *confirming* your *bias*). For example, people who believe flying in airplanes is dangerous (even though studies disagree) often spend hours performing online searches of all the airplane crashes in history, and each time they

PLANNING FALLACY

Similar to the finished-product bias, the planning fallacy is the tendency to underestimate the amount of time needed to learn a new skill (often causing you to feel disappointed in your progress). When you remind yourself that it takes a long time to make something look easy, you can avoid much of the disappointment the planning fallacy can make you feel. ●

read of another, they *confirm* their own *bias* a little more. Not surprisingly, these people rarely search the safety records of airlines because that would contradict their bias. You can avoid confirmation bias by reminding yourself that it's all right to be wrong sometimes. The next time you're given the chance to try something new, remember that being right all the time isn't worth making a wrong decision even one time.

●●● Blind-Spot Biases and Out-Grouping

The only way to remove the burden created by a *blind-spot bias* is to become mindful of it. Much like the vehicle hidden in your car's blind spot, as soon as you're aware of it (as soon as it leaves your blind spot), the threat it creates goes away. But there's another problem with blind-spot biases and it's their connection to *out-grouping* (comparing yourself to others, body envy, and shame)!

Think about it for a minute. Do any of these blind-spot biases sound familiar? If so, perhaps it's because most of them contain thoughts of out-grouping!

For example:

- *Bandwagon Bias*: You lose your individuality by always adopting the beliefs of *others*.

- *Self-Serving Bias*: You blame bad things on *others* so you feel better about yourself.

- *Bad-Guy Bias*: You worry that *others* are saying bad things about you.

- *Spotlight Bias*: You get anxious because you think *others* are always watching you.

- *Finished-Product Bias*: You compare yourself to or are envious of *others*.

Earlier in this book, I made a bold statement saying you can eliminate the majority of wondering, wishing, and worrying by simply eliminating out-grouping. I hope  that's becoming even clearer now. Out-grouping forms the very foundation of most blind-spot biases and *limiting beliefs*! Remove out-grouping and you remove blind-spot biases. Remove blind-spot biases and you remove limiting beliefs. Remove limiting beliefs and you remove your limits! ●

TRUE STORY

Confirmation bias exists at the barn too. A rider in a recent clinic entered my arena on a very forward and unmanageable horse. After observing the horse, I asked, "How long have you been trying to slow your horse?" to which she replied, "Four years!" So, I suggested she try something new. "Instead of slowing your horse," I said, "Try calming your horse." After all, doing the same thing over and over again and expecting a different result is a bit insane. I then instructed her to give her horse five calming aids: soften her hands, use a calming voice, relax her hips, use calming circles, and take her weight off his back (she was in a chair seat). To this, she simply replied, "It'll never work," to which I replied, "Never tell yourself what you can't do until you at least try."

Unconvinced it would work, she picked up the canter, but as soon as her horse sped up, she thought about it for a second, then abruptly threw her reins away and thrust herself forward causing her horse to bolt and run away. After a few minutes of leaning back and yanking on her horse's mouth, she came to me and said the five words I knew she'd say, "See I told you so!" ●

★ MORAL OF THE STORY:

This rider had a belief that you can only slow horses by leaning back and pulling, and confirmed it by acting in a way that would ensure it happened. But here's the sad part. When she confirmed her bias, she missed the opportunity to solve a problem that had plagued her and her horse for years. In the end, her desire to be right was stronger than her desire to improve the relationship with her horse.

– Recognize Blind-Spot Bias Exercise –

Bring your blind-spot biases out into the light by recognizing them. Make a list of any biases you might have used in the past, describe them, and then place a checkmark in the column I.C.U. (I see you!) and be thankful it's no longer hidden in your blind spot. If you can see it, you can solve it!

☆ Bias	☆ Description	☆ I.C.U
....	....	....
....	....	....
....	....	....
....	....	....
....	....	....
....	....	....
....	....	....
....	....	....
....	....	....
....	....	....
....	....	....
....	....	....
....	....	....
....	....	....
....	....	....

YOUR MIND IS LIKE
A PARACHUTE. IT ONLY WORKS
WHEN IT'S OPEN.

4

chapter

minding your mindsets

4

chapter

You're not supposed to just go through life, you're supposed to *grow* through life, and developing a self-confident and empowering mindset is how you achieve it. Your mindset determines how you act, what you believe, how you treat yourself (and others), and who you'll ultimately become. It determines who *you* are and is the very fabric of everything you do and everything you believe. From what drives you to what scares you, and from how you approach challenges to how you recover from them, mindset is everything. Your thoughts, beliefs, attitude, and aptitude are all determined by your mindset. It's the truest reflection of who you are, and all the personal qualities that make you unique and valuable. Being *bold, brave* and *bright* is a mindset.

●●● Qualities of a Healthy Mindset

There are many different mindsets. Some raise you up while others weigh you down. Some help you grow while others make you feel like your potential is fixed. Becoming mindful of these mindsets can empower you to select and create the ones that raise you up so you can grow through life. Before I introduce the different mindsets, I'd like to first tell you about the five positive basic qualities that create any healthy mindset:

Never underestimate the power of persistence. It's what stands between a rock and a hard place.

●● { 1 } Persistence

This is the quality of never quitting regardless of struggles or setbacks. It's the ability to keep striving for your goals, hold it together when it would be normal to fall apart, and finish what you start.

don't quit

If there's a problem and solution, there's no problem.

●● { 2 } Positive Realism

Positive is good, but being realistic is just as important. An overinflated mindset can get you into trouble because not all situations are going to be 100 percent positive. Making the best of a bad situation without losing confidence is the key to *positive realism*.

MINDSET BY THE NUMBER

If

A, B, C, D, E, F, G, H, I, J, K, L, M, N, O, P, Q, R, S, T, U, V, W, X, Y, Z

equal

1, 2, 3, 4, 5, 6, 7, 8, 9, 10, 11, 12, 13, 14, 15, 16, 17, 18, 19, 20, 21, 22, 23, 24, 25, 26%

then

KNOWLEDGE = 96%
(11, 14, 15, 25, 12, 5, 4, 7, 5)

and

HARD WORK = 98%
(8, 1, 18, 4, 23, 15, 18, 11)

Both are important, but

ATTITUDE = 100%!
(1, 20, 20, 9, 20, 21, 4, 5)

●● { 3 } Humility

Riders with *humility* have a desire to improve and are confident in their abilities, but also assess their strengths and weaknesses without under- or overestimating them. They know hard work can change weaknesses into strengths, but that it takes time, effort, and courage.

●● { 4 } Vulnerability

Riders who allow themselves to be *vulnerable*, don't dwell on mistakes or failures because they know they can learn as much from them as they do from their successes. They're not afraid to try new things, admit they have more to learn, or ask for help.

●● { 5 } No Regrets

Regret is one of the most destructive of all emotions because it casts a shadow of doubt over your abilities, and causes you to lose faith in yourself. Riders  *without regret* feel periodic disappointment, but they never allow it to sidetrack their efforts or confidence.

Now that you know what creates a healthy and empowered mindset, let's talk about how these five qualities come together to create the first two mindsets.

●●● Growth vs. Fixed Mindsets

Riders with a *growth mindset* believe that talent can grow with time and experience. To these riders, skill is just a starting point that can be enhanced with the right amount of effort, practice, and repetition. Riders with a growth mindset know their potential is nearly limitless, and that they (and no one else) control how successful they'll become. They thrive on challenges and love to stretch outside their comfort zone. While they don't believe everyone is the same, they do believe that everyone can grow and evolve if they're only willing to put in a little time and effort.

> Never limit your challenges. Challenge your limits.

When it comes to the five *positive-mindset* qualities just outlined above, riders with a *growth mindset* are persistent and act with positive realism and humility. They also allow themselves to feel vulnerable from time to time, and live life in such a way that they rarely experience regret.

Riders with a *fixed mindset*, on the other hand, believe that talent is a fixed trait that cannot change. They feel they're born with a certain amount of skill and no matter what they do they can never change or improve it. These riders believe that talent is predetermined, so they rarely attempt to improve it. As a result, they often avoid challenges because it's the only way to avoid making mistakes. They also believe that only skill leads to success, and that effort is bad or even embarrassing (after all, talented riders shouldn't have to make an effort!). As a result, these riders shy away from challenges and/or give up altogether if there's a risk of failure.

When it comes to the five *positive-mindset* qualities mentioned earlier, riders with a fixed mindset tend to be quick quitters, struggle mak-

ing the best of a bad situation, and lack belief in their abilities. They also tend to see vulnerability as a weakness and experience frequent regret.

TRUE STORY

An appreciative teacher offered his entire class a B on their final exam without even asking them to write it. Many of the students happily accepted the B and left the room. Those who stayed to write the test were pleasantly surprised when they turned their test papers over to see the words, "Congratulations for not settling. You just earned an A." ●

★ MORAL OF THE STORY:

Never settle in life. Always believe you're capable of an A.

*Do what you can,
with what you have,
where you are.*

- THEODORE ROOSEVELT -
US President,
Conservationist,
Naturalist

●●● **Effort Vision**

In addition to the ideas that skills and talent can either grow or are fixed, riders with the *growth* or *fixed mindset* also differ in how they view *effort*. This is called *effort vision*. Riders with a growth-mindset believe success doesn't happen automatically; you have to work hard for it by thinking bigger, taking risks,

Ready, set, grow!

Good things
come to those
who wait.
Better things
come to those
who try.

SETBACKS
TO COMEBACKS

One of the best feelings in the world is turning a setback into a comeback, and in doing so proving that a little resiliency can lead to big rewards. Sadly, riders with a fixed mindset never get to experience these rewards because they usually quit before the comeback part. ●

and making an effort regardless of the outcome. These riders enjoy the journey, not just the destination. Riders with a fixed mindset, on the other hand, believe success should occur without effort. They feel they were born with a certain amount of talent and if they don't succeed, it's simply because they weren't given enough. They focus almost entirely on outcomes, feeling that if they're not the best, it's been a waste of time. These riders focus so much on the destination that they rarely enjoy the journey.

Water at 211 degrees Fahrenheit is just hot. But add just one more degree and it can power a train! Talent is the train and effort is the extra degree that powers it. ▶

The *fixed* and *growth mindsets* don't act alone. In fact, they're made up of many other closely related mindsets that combine together to create them. Just like the fixed and growth mindsets, these other mindsets have two sides: one good and one evil. Here are sixteen such mindsets:

●● The Victim and the Survivor Mindsets

Riders with a *victim mindset* think life's unfair and there's nothing they can do about it (so why even try). This mindset is also called *learned helplessness* because these riders have learned to feel helpless; to believe they're just victims of their circumstances and nothing they do will make any difference. Riders with a *survivor mindset*, however, don't believe they're victims, but instead relish the opportunity to find solutions to curious challenges. To these riders, obstacles aren't problems that need to be avoided, but questions that beg to be answered. Hard work is their greatest tool as they define themselves by the efforts they make, not the outcomes they receive. Feeling like

---

TRUE STORY

One fisherman noticed another doing something unusual. Every time he caught a small fish, he'd keep it, and every time he caught a large one he'd throw it back. Finding this peculiar he asked, "Why do you only keep the small ones?" to which the fisherman replied, "I only have a small frying pan. The big ones don't fit, so I have to throw them back." ●

★ MORAL OF THE STORY:

Get a bigger frying pan! Your life is like this story. It's full of large opportunities that don't fit in a small frying pan (fixed mindset). Instead of throwing them away, get a bigger frying pan (growth mindset) so you can keep all your hard-earned fish!

> The survivor mindset
> is like wrestling a gorilla.
> You don't quit when you're tired.
> You quit when the gorilla is tired.

a victim is a part of the fixed mindset. Feeling like a survivor is part of the growth mindset.

●● The Scarcity and the Abundance Mindsets

Riders with the *scarcity mindset* tend to focus on what they don't have (like a good equitation or fancy horse) and believe they don't have enough talent or time to get it. These riders spend so much time focusing on what's scarce (not having enough or not being enough) that they forget to try to make things better. Riders with an *abundance mindset*, however, focus on what they do have, but instead of thinking in terms of equitation and fancy horses, they think in terms of time and effort—knowing that

TRUE STORY

A young boy throws a base-ball up into the air, swings at it, and misses. Strike one. Undeterred, he picks the ball up, throws it up again, swings and misses a second time. Strike two. Never the quitter, he throws it up a third time, swings with all his might, and misses again. Strike three. His mother (who's been watching) fears he'll feel sad so asks him if he feels bad. "Bad?" he replies with surprise. "Why would I feel bad? I've become such an amazing pitcher I can't even hit my own pitches!" ●

★ MORAL OF THE STORY:

Mindsets are like this boy. The negative is often easier to see, but the positive will show itself if you just keep swinging!

they have an abundance of both. Scarcity is part of the fixed mindset. Abundance is part of the growth mindset.

The Self- and the Selfless Mindsets

Riders with a *self-mindset* feel threatened when others do well and struggle feeling happy for them when they do. They also tend to have fragile egos, which makes it hard for them to share the credit with anyone when they succeed (like their coach or teammates). To these riders, it's all about *them*. Rider with a *selfless mindset*, however, aren't threatened by the success of others. Instead of feeling jealousy or envy, they feel genuine happiness for that person, knowing their success doesn't detract from their own. These riders take pride in their success, but also take pride in sharing the credit with their coaches and teammates. *Self* is part of the fixed mindset. *Selfless* is part of the growth mindset.

> When a storm hits, eagles set their wings and fly above it. Instead of trying to escape the storm, they use it to rise higher. Be an eagle!

The Short-Term and the Long-Term Mindsets

Just because you don't succeed today doesn't mean you can't succeed tomorrow. Riders with a *short-term mindset* struggle with this concept because they base their self-image on a single moment in time (especially if that moment is disappointing). These riders only set short-term goals because long-term goals require greater effort and risk, and as a result they usually only experience short-term happiness. Riders with a *long-term mindset*, however, know that success isn't created on a single day or in a single class, but instead over a lifetime of

START WITH SMALL

US Navy Four-Star Admiral William McRaven famously said, "When you make your bed every morning, you will have accomplished the first task of the day. It will give you a small sense of pride and encourage you to do another task and another task. If you aren't willing to make the small efforts, how can you expect to be able to make the big ones?"

hard work. These riders know that focusing on the short term alone can have long-term consequences. Short term is part of the fixed mindset. Long term is part of the growth mindset.

You earn your ribbons in your lessons. You just pick them up at the shows!

The Dread and the Dreamer Mindsets

There's a little bit of the *dread mindset* in everyone. It's where *wondering*, *wishing*, and *worrying* lives. It's the fear that you'll do your best, but your best won't be good enough. Riders who constantly focus on dread, however, convince themselves that the challenges are bigger than their abilities. As a result, they tend to avoid making an effort because they're pretty sure it won't be enough. Riders with a *dreamer mindset*, on the other hand, dream big and think big, but also put in big efforts. They believe most things are possible and aren't afraid of setting meaningful goals that can make their dreams come true. Dread is part of the fixed mindset. Dreams are part of the growth mindset.

> Challenges are what make riding so interesting. Overcoming them is what makes riding so rewarding.

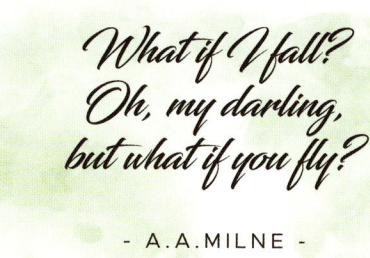

What if I fall?
Oh, my darling,
but what if you fly?

- A.A.MILNE -
Author

When NASA selects its astronauts, they don't search for people who've always succeeded in life. Instead, they seek candidates who've gone through struggles but never gave up on themselves, their goals, or their dreams.

●● The Fear
and the Feedback Mindsets

Riders with a *fear mindset* live with a *what-if* and *not-enough* mentality. "*What if* I'm *not good enough*, or *what if* I try hard but it's *not enough*?" For the most part, these riders focus so much on the negative things that *might* happen in the future that they're incapable of enjoying the positive things they can create in the present. Riders with a *feedback mindset*, however, live with a *so-what-if* and an *it's-enough* mentality. They don't worry about things that might happen in the future, but use feedback from those situations to improve. To these riders, "What if I lose?" turns into, "*So what if* I lose, *it's enough* that I tried and learned." Fear is part of the fixed mindset. Feedback is part of the growth mindset.

●● The Win
and the Winning Mindsets

Riders with a *win mindset* see winning as an all-or-nothing proposition. They either win or

93

Hedonic Adaptation

Researchers found that when you meet your desire to have more success, you'll quickly return to the same level of happiness you had before it. This is why it's so common for some riders to continually want more, and to be continually disappointed with what they have (even when they have more than before). You can overcome hedonic adaptation by always reminding yourself how lucky you are to have what you have!

The only negative thing I want in my life is a Coggins test!

they're losers. Even second place to them is reserved for the first loser. These riders struggle with losing and let it harm their self-image every time they come up short. Since they're unable to accept losses, they tend to deflect responsibility by blaming it on the footing, judge, or horse, for example. Riders with a *winning mindset*, however, don't define winning and losing as opposites. To them, both are learning opportunities, and while they certainly enjoy the wins, they also take pride in learning from their losses. Win is part of the fixed mindset. Winning is part of the growth mindset.

The Greed and the Gratitude Mindsets

Riders with a *greed mindset* struggle to be thankful for what they have because they're always so busy wanting more. Instead of being satisfied and enjoying their horse, tack, and trailer, they feel resentful because they wish they had fancier, nicer, and bigger. In other words, these riders feel bad because they don't *have* what they

– Are You Fixed or Growing Exercise –

Consider the following statements and which are true about you:

☆ Fixed Mindset

You try to hide flaws so you won't be labeled a failure.

You avoid challenges so you can avoid making mistakes.

You think that failing means you're a failure.

You think making an effort means you're untalented.

When you fail you think you've wasted your time.

When bad things happen you feel helpless to change them.

You feel threatened when others do well.

You think you're born with a set amount of talent.

☆ Growth Mindset

You view flaws as a to-do list of things to improve.

You seek challenges so you can learn from them.

You think that failing means you have more to learn.

You think effort is the key to achievement.

When you fail you think you just learned something.

When bad things happen you find a way to make them better.

You feel genuinely happy for others when they succeed.

You think hard work and effort can make your talent grow.

Being Fateful at Being Grateful

What do you think of when you think of the barn? Are you reminded how the smell of horses brings a rush of calm over your body? Do you recall how excited you were the first time you swung your leg over the saddle? Can you remember the first time you heard a nicker when you walked through the barn and how it put a smile on your face?

Gratitude helps you experience compassion, happiness, and joy. Creating a gratitude-list is a great way to help notice what's already good in your life. It's an immediate perspective shift. It allows you to take a step back, find your joy, and make every moment with your horse a memorable one.

The next time you step into the barn ask yourself, "What am I grateful for?" and simply notice the shift in your mood and the smile it brings to your face. ●

Great riders don't just go through life—they grow through life!

want. Riders with a *gratitude mindset*, however, tend to be happier because they *want* everything they *have*. They know that fancier, nicer, and bigger exist (and love it when they receive them) but don't spend every waking minute hoping for them. These riders don't take what they have for granted, but instead, appreciate everything they've been given. Greed is part of the fixed mindset. Gratitude is part of the growth mindset.

●●● Fixing the Fixed Mindset

Even if you have a few fixed-mindset tendencies, never give up! The fixed mindset isn't fixed either. It can grow as long as you believe it. The first step is to commit to changing your beliefs about what you're capable of accomplishing. If you can learn to believe that your abilities, skills, and talents aren't fixed, you might just find yourself seeking out situations that will

NEVER *give up*

help you to grow. Reflect on the five qualities of a healthy mindset, and the eight mindsets that contribute to growth, and you'll be well on your way to going from fixed to growth. ●

Don't think outside the box.

Think like there is no box.

97

– Unfixing the Fixed

If you'd like a little more help you can give

☆ **Remind yourself** you're a survivor by writing two challenging obstacles you've overcome:

A: ....

B: ....

☆ **Remind yourself** you're capable and talented by writing two skills you're good at:

A: ....

B: ....

☆ **Remind yourself** you're not selfish by writing two times you felt happy for the success of others:

A: ....

B: ....

☆ **Remind yourself** you're willing to take risks by writing two long-terms goals you've achieved:

A: ....

B: ....

Mindset Exercise –

the following worksheet a try:

☆ **Remind yourself** it's okay to be a dreamer by writing two long-term goals you'd love to achieve:

A: ....

B: ....

☆ **Remind yourself** that feedback is valuable by writing two things you've learned from failures:

A: ....

B: ....

☆ **Remind yourself** of a winning mindset by writing two times you lost, but felt like a winner:

A: ....

B: ....

☆ **Remind yourself** that you don't have a greed mindset by writing two things you're grateful for:

A: ....

B: ....

RIDERS NEVER STOP
LEARNING BECAUSE
HORSES NEVER STOP
TEACHING.

5

chapter

neuroplasticity

5

chapter

Not long ago it was thought the human brain finished growing by the age of three, but modern imaging technology has proven that your brain is actually capable of growing (and even changing its shape) well into adulthood. Regardless of whether it's learning to ride a horse or speak a new language, your brain is capable of growing and changing just like you are. This is called neuroplasticity, "neuroelasticity," or neurogenesis and provides scientific proof that the *growth mindset* (p. 83) is real.

Your brain has billions of neurons, each with thousands of connections to other neurons. They meet at *synapses* and communicate via neurotransmitters, which ulti- 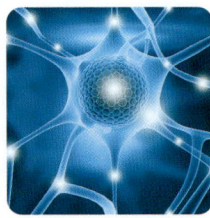 mately create your thoughts, skills, and behaviors. Every time you have a new experience, your brain creates

TRUE STORY

London taxi drivers undergo intensive training to memorize the thousands of complex city streets. Musicians dedicate endless hours learning their instruments. Perhaps it's no surprise that MRIs have found larger-than-average memory centers in the brains of London cab drivers and larger-than-average auditory centers in the brains of musicians. ●

★ MORAL OF THE STORY:

Your brain is like a muscle. The more you use certain parts, the more they grow!

new connections between them, and every time you have that same experience again, your brain strengthens those connections. In time, these connections become *wired* together, much

like a forest path that gets more defined over time. Eventually, these *wired connections* allow skills and behaviors to become automatic (muscle memory) because when one fires, so does the other. In other words, neurons that get wired together get fired together.

●●● The Anxiety Cycle Is Not a Spinning Class!

So, what does neuroplasticity have to do with becoming *bolder, braver,* and *brighter*? Well, overcoming emotional challenges like anxiety, show jitters, and out-grouping is a skill, and like any skill, you can improve it by practicing and learning to *wire* the correct neurons together. But in order for this to happen, you must first overcome something called the *anxiety cycle.*

The *anxiety cycle* works like this: When you avoid something scary, your brain releases a surge of relief that makes you feel better, which increases the likelihood of your brain telling you to avoid other scary things in the future. Every time you avoid something scary and survive, your brain links together more neurons that strengthen that habit, even if the scary thing

Sometimes, you're just going to have to "do it afraid."

isn't dangerous (like backing up a trailer, for example). Before long, the anxiety cycle creates neural connections that make you avoid situations that might seem scary. Every time you avoid something scary and survive, your

brain says, "Yay, let's always do that!" Eventually, it becomes a habit because your brain wires *scary* and *avoidance* together (wired together and fired together).

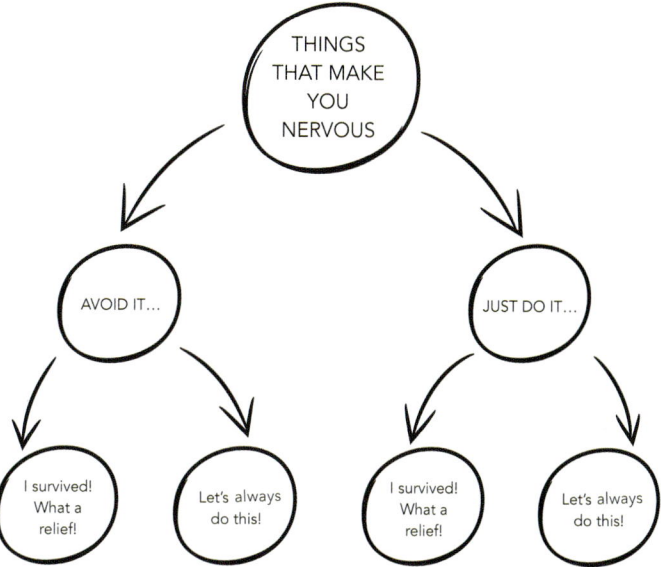

The trick to overcoming the anxiety cycle is to just do those things that feel a bit scary (just back up the trailer already!). If you do them and don't die (spoiler alert: you won't) your brain says, "What a relief!"

and will begin breaking the neural connections between scary and avoidance, and begin building new connections between scary and safe. In the end, neuroplasticity is what helps you to break the anxiety cycle, and breaking the anxiety cycle is what helps you to become *bolder, braver,* and *brighter.*

●●● The Learning Ladder

Making anything look easy is hard because creating bold neuronal connections takes time. That's why effort and errors are so important to learning. When a mistake occurs, your brain simply says, "Well, that didn't work so I won't wire and fire those neurons together again." Having the *patience* to wait, and the *trust* to believe this, are the keys to leaning any new mental or physical skill.

Luckily, the process of acquiring new skills follows four pretty predictable stages. Knowing what they are (and what you should expect to *feel* during each stage) can relieve much of the anxiety you might experience. It can also help you to manage your expectations, maintain motivation, and avoid thinking self-defeating thoughts.

Unconscious Incompetence > *Conscious Incompetence* > *Conscious Competence* > *Unconscious Competence*

| *You are unaware of the skill and you lack proficiency* | *You are aware of the skill but are not yet proficient* | *You are able to use the skill but only with effort* | *Performing the skill becomes automatic* |

The *learning ladder* is a four-step program designed to help you understand the natural thoughts and emotions that can occur when learning a new skill. As you'll see, some stages are fun while others are frustrating, but all

You have to eat all those peas before you can get to that chocolate pudding. Don't worry, you'll learn to like peas.

You have to eat all that fence before you can get to that green grass. Don't worry, you'll learn to like fences.

four stages focus on two important factors: consciousness (awareness) and skill (competence).

Stage One: Unconsciously Incompetent (Not Knowing What You Don't Know)

I didn't realize I was supposed to know how to do everything by my second rodeo. Seems like a very low number of rodeos...

You're blissfully ignorant during this stage. You're new to the skill and don't feel bad not knowing what you're doing, because you've never done it before! It's new and unique and exciting, and your expectations are low or even nonexistent. You don't compare yourself to others or worry you're not good enough. You're

Don't know what you don't know

simply happy because you're taking part in the activity. This is called the *autotelic experience* (p. 234) and is what makes the unconsciously incompetent stage fun, carefree, and enjoyable.

107

My daughter Emma's expression while in the first stage of learning!

This first stage is defined by *not knowing what you don't know*. You don't know that you don't know how to do the skill. You're just happy you're doing it! Sometimes your confidence can exceed your ability here, so it's important to listen to your trainer and behave safely. Unfortunately, very little learning happens during this stage (that begins in the next stage) so welcoming new challenges and building a desire to grow and improve are important to moving on to the next level.

Stage Two:
Consciously Incompetent
(Knowing What You Don't Know)

This is the most difficult and disheartening stage of learning because it's here that you realize you don't have a skill you wish you had. Even worse, you become acutely aware that other riders can do that skill (and even make it look easy!).

As a result, out-grouping usually begins when you enter this stage because you're given irrefutable proof that other riders are better than you. You'll likely also experience a little disappointment, defeat, and dejection during this stage because your efforts won't

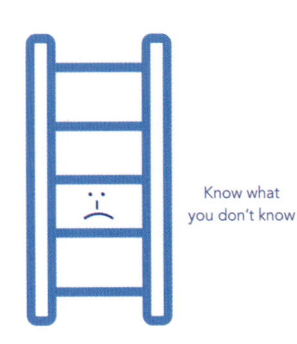

Know what you don't know

always match up with the demands of the skill. You'll put the effort in, but the desired results won't always come out. As a result, it's quite common to feel a bit frustrated and cranky (or what I like to call *FRANKY*). This is the stage of learning where the fear of failure, perfectionism, and defense mechanisms also usually begin.

Frustrated
+
Cranky
=
FRANKY

This stage is defined by *knowing what you don't know,* and by the words "consciously incompetent," alone, it's easy to see why this phase can be so emotionally difficult. After all, in the first stage you were oblivious to your weaknesses and shortcomings, but in this phase you know exactly what they are! This stage is, however, critical to your development because it's here that your efforts and errors begin to form the important neutral connections that'll ultimately make the skill possible. Without this phase, there can be no growth and no continued movement up the ladder. But there's a problem: Many riders get so disheartened during this stage that they stop (quit) before they can step up to the next rung of the *learning ladder.*

I've learned that I have a lot to learn. It's been lovely but I have to scream now.

109

Confidence
won't
make it easy.
It will make
it possible.

Stage Three: Consciously Competent (Knowing What You Know)

This stage is going to feel a whole lot better than the second stage, because it's here that all your hard work and patience finally begin to pay off.

It's during this stage that your previous efforts and errors give rise to the understanding of the skill, because the important neural connections have now been wired together.

Know what you know

This stage is defined by *knowing what you know.* You now know what needs to be done, when it needs to be done—and you can actually do it! It's during this stage that you realize you're capable of doing something that (until recently) you were incapable of achieving. Making the impossible possible is what makes this stage so rewarding. But this stage is only made possible because of tough lessons learned in Stage Two. Without them, the impossible would still be impossible. It's important to remember that while you're now competent at the new skill, it still

*Perseverance is the hard work you do
after you get tired of doing
the hard work you already did.*

- NEWT GINGRICH -
Politician

requires effort, and periodic errors will still occur, but with continued practice and patience, you'll continue to gain more proficiency, and eventually make the skill feel practically automatic (muscle memory).

Stage Four: Unconsciously Competent (Not Knowing What You Know)

When you arrive at this stage, you're no longer even aware you possess a particular skill. It's become so automatic and natural that you perform it effortlessly without any real conscious thought or effort. You don't even think about it—it just happens! It's now *muscle memory.* The important neural connections have been wired together and they get firing together subconsciously. You feel completely confident with the skill and are no longer *wondering, wishing,* or *worrying* about it, which is wonderful because you had to go through a couple of pretty tough stages to get there. This stage is defined by *not knowing what you know.* You know so much stuff that you don't even know it!

Don't know what
you know

Becoming mindful of the Four Stages of the learning ladder can *help* relieve much of the disappointment you might otherwise feel when attempting new skills, *help*

COACHES' CORNER

The learning ladder can help coaches understand what their students might be thinking and experiencing as they learn new skills. It also helps trainers design specific programs with reasonable exceptions and exercises based on the exact stage of learning for each of their riders. ●

you understand the emotions you're likely to experience along the way, and *help* you maintain motivation throughout the four-stage journey. This is yet another example of how *helpful* mindfulness can be. Here's a story that can *help* you understand the four-stage learning ladder a little better:

• STAGE ONE: **Unconsciously Incompetent (Not Knowing What You Don't Know)** —Imagine a young rider just starting out. Every second spent at the barn is exciting and new. When she's not at the barn, she can't stop thinking about being there, and when she's at the barn she can't stop thinking of ways to never leave it. She happily jumps on the back of her pony and giggles her way around the arena, knowing that riding, and that fat pony, are the best things that have ever happened to her.

QUESTION: *Does she worry about her posting-trot diagonals?*

ANSWER: *No…because she doesn't even know they exist!*

As a result, she doesn't feel bad about not knowing her diagonals because *she doesn't know what she doesn't know!* This is a super fun stage. No *wondering, wishing,* and *worrying* here.

• STAGE TWO: **Consciously Incompetent (Knowing What You Don't Know)** —Now imagine that this young rider arrives at the barn one day, but her trainer says, "Today we're going to learn something called posting-trot diagonals." This is the day that her riding emotions might take a bit of a turn. Imagine that no matter how hard she tries, she just can't seem to see her diagonals (or even grasp what they really mean). She

113

Good enough
has been good
enough for
long enough.
Take it to the
next level.

does her best, but her best isn't good enough. She feels disappointed and upset, begins to doubt herself, and starts comparing herself to other riders ("Everyone can do it except me!"). She even starts to lie to her trainer about being able to see her diagonals (it's a 50/50 chance!) because she doesn't want him to think she's incompetent. She becomes frustrated and cranky (FRANKY!), and for the first time, riding starts to feel more frustrating than fun. All because she now *knows what she doesn't know.*

- **STAGE THREE:** **Consciously Competent (Knowing What You Know)** —Even though the bright and carefree emotions of her initial riding experiences have changed to something darker, she doesn't quit or give up. She trusts her trainer and reminds herself she's capable of accomplishing difficult tasks, so she continues to do her best—and one day, she finally learns her diagonals! Proud of herself, and equally thankful the struggle is over, she now *knows what she knows* (her diagonals)!

115

Ferg**U**s BY JEAN ABERNETHY

Sure, you may be out there laughing at what a bad horse I am, and how you wouldn't put up with this... ...but you have to admit...

...by the time this kid is grown up, she'll be one heck of a horsewoman!

© ABERNETHY 2011

- **STAGE FOUR:** **Unconsciously Competent (Not Knowing What You Know)** —Inspired by her efforts and progress, the girl continues to focus on her diagonals until the time comes that seeing them is completely natural and automatic, even to the point where she no longer needs to look for them. She can simply feel them and change automatically whenever needed. The important neural connections have now been wired together (and fired together) without her even knowing it. She now *doesn't even know what she knows!*

●●● FRANKY Climbs the Ladder

One of the most important takeaways from the *learning ladder* is that *FRANKY* is a part of your future. Every time you embark on the journey to learn a new skill, there's a chance you might feel a bit frustrated and cranky. Not because you're incapable of doing the task, but because you're simply not capable of doing it *yet*. That will come farther up the ladder. You'll struggle and fail and fail again, but with a little courage and self-belief, you'll soon move past the *FRANKY* phase and onto the other more enjoyable steps of the ladder.

It goes without saying that you'll want to speed through the *FRANKY* stage as fast as you can, but the amount of time you spend there is actually up to you. It comes down to a willingness to make the effort and the errors, and to learn from each one of them. Remember, every time you make a mistake, your brain will say, "Okay, that didn't work. I won't wire or fire those neurons together again." Learning a skill like riding isn't easy, but a willingness to make the effort and the errors is what'll make it possible.

The amount of time you spend in the *FRANKY* stage is also directly related to your willingness to be vulnerable (to try new things and push yourself outside your comfort zone). If you're afraid to try new things or afraid of being vulnerable, it's going to be difficult to move beyond the *FRANKY* stage of the *learning ladder*.

●●● Vulnerability

While vulnerability is often misinterpreted as a sign of weakness, it's actually the complete opposite. Allowing yourself to be vulnerable is a sign of courage! After all, it doesn't take any courage to say you're *never* afraid or that you *never* struggle. Anyone can do that. What takes courage is having the self-confidence to admit that sometimes you do feel a bit fearful, frustrated, or vulnerable. Riders who won't admit that are usually just too afraid to admit it! Allowing yourself to be vulnerable (by accepting your faults and flaws) is a sign of courage and is what will make you *bolder, braver,* and *brighter.*

Consider the story of the rider who struggled learning her diagonals. There came a time when she began to lie to her trainer about her ability to see her diagonals. As you can imagine, that only prolonged the amount of time she remained in the *FRANKY* stage (the longer she lied about it, the longer she went without help), but if she had summoned up the courage to be vulnerable and admitted her shortcomings earlier (by asking for more help), she'd have surely learned her diagonals quicker, and moved beyond the *FRANKY* stage faster.

To admit your weaknesses is to make yourself vulnerable. To make yourself vulnerable is to take a risk. Taking a risk requires courage. Vulnerability is, therefore, proof that you're brave.

TRUE STORY

Did you know a lobster's body grows throughout its life, but its shell does not? As a result, a lobster must make a difficult decision: live with the increasing pressure of living in a shell that's too confining, or shed the shell so it can grow a bigger one. The only problem is, when a lobster molts and wiggles out of its shell (which it does five to seven times in its life) it becomes a defenseless piece of meat lying on the ocean floor while it grows its new shell. Lobsters have figured out, however, that in order to grow, they must have the courage to be vulnerable (even if it means becoming a tasty meal for the next passing sea creature). Lobsters have developed a growth mindset. They know that growth only comes to those who are willing to be vulnerable, and to those who are willing to shed their shells. ●

★ MORAL OF THE STORY:

Live life like a lobster!

There's no escaping the fact that you're going to feel a little *FRANKY* sometimes. It's a part of every *learning ladder*. When challenges make you feel frustrated and cranky, remind yourself that you're just in *that* stage of learning (just at that rung of the ladder) and that all the other amaz-

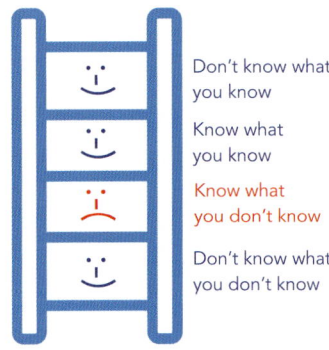

Don't know what
you know

Know what
you know

Know what
you don't know

Don't know what
you don't know

ing stages of learning are waiting for you. As long as you have the courage to make the effort and the errors, and to be vulnerable, you'll get to the top of every ladder you ever climb. ●

Climbing the Ladder Exercise

*Make your way to the top of your learning ladder
by taking one confident step at a time. You might encounter
a period that feels a little FRANKY, but never lose faith
and never stop climbing. Here's an exercise that can help you
get to the top of any learning ladder you ever climb:*

☆ Write a skill that's in the second (FRANKY) stage of your learning ladder. This is a skill you're working hard to acquire, but can't quite seem to make it happen:

....

....

☆ Write a skill you can do naturally and without effort (a skill on the top rung of your ladder):

....

....

☆ Fill in the ladder below with examples of the kinds of thoughts you experienced during each step while learning this top-rung skill:

Top rung: .... *(You don't know what you now know.)*

Third rung: .... *(You knew what you knew.)*

Second rung: .... *(You knew what you didn't know.)*

Bottom rung: .... *(You didn't know what you didn't know.)*

☆ Look back to the first skill (the one you can't do yet) and use information from Step 3 to prove that you can reach any goal you set your mind to do, as long as you're willing to make an effort, accept a few errors, and feel a bit vulnerable from time to time. When it happens, just keep climbing!

2

EQUESTRIANS DON'T MAKE MISTAKES. MISTAKES MAKE EQUESTRIANS *BOLDER, BRAVER,* AND *BRIGHTER.*

PART TWO

braver

braver

You aren't going to get through life unscathed: you'll fall, fail, fear, freak out, and get *FRANKY* from time to time, but it's far better to accept and overcome these struggles than it is to dwell on them, try to cover them up, or hope they'll never happen (spoiler alert—they will!). This is the essence of bravery—knowing that sometimes you might just have to do it when you are afraid.

So, what does it really mean to be brave? Does it mean you'll never worry or doubt yourself? Does it mean you'll never fail or be afraid again? No. Being brave doesn't mean you'll never struggle or stumble again, it simply means that when it happens, you'll have the courage to cope, recover, and go forward, regardless of what's trying to hold you

BRAVE

The quality of having the courage to push through fears and failures without losing hope and to emerge stronger, more focused, more engaged, and more committed than ever.●

back. Courage isn't the absence of fear. It's the presence of fear, but doing it anyway (as long as it doesn't endanger your safety).

Being brave is to accept the fact that sometimes there might just be a little bitter before the sweet.

Some riders believe that only success breeds success, but in fact, struggles play an even greater role developing courage. It's the lessons learned and toughness earned that can only come from falling short or falling off, which creates the grit and resiliency that'll take you toward courage. Believing there's just as much education in your failures as there are in

YOU ARE

BRAVER
THAN YOU BELIEVE

STRONGER
THAN YOU SEEM

SMARTER
THAN YOU THINK

AND

LOVED
MORE THAN YOU'LL EVER KNOW

♡ WINNIE THE POOH

Courage doesn't mean you won't fall down or fall behind. It means you'll do those things without falling apart.

your victories is what really creates brave riders. Without a periodic slip-up or snafu, your riding experiences would be devoid of learning opportunities. Your mistakes, mess-ups, and missed opportunities aren't the opposite of bravery, they're a part of it! ●

Courage
puts you
where good
luck can
find you.

TALENT WON'T OPEN DOORS FOR YOU, BUT IT'LL UNLOCK THEM. ALL YOU HAVE TO DO IS HAVE THE COURAGE TO PUSH THEM OPEN.

chapter 6

fight, flight, freeze, freak out, and forget

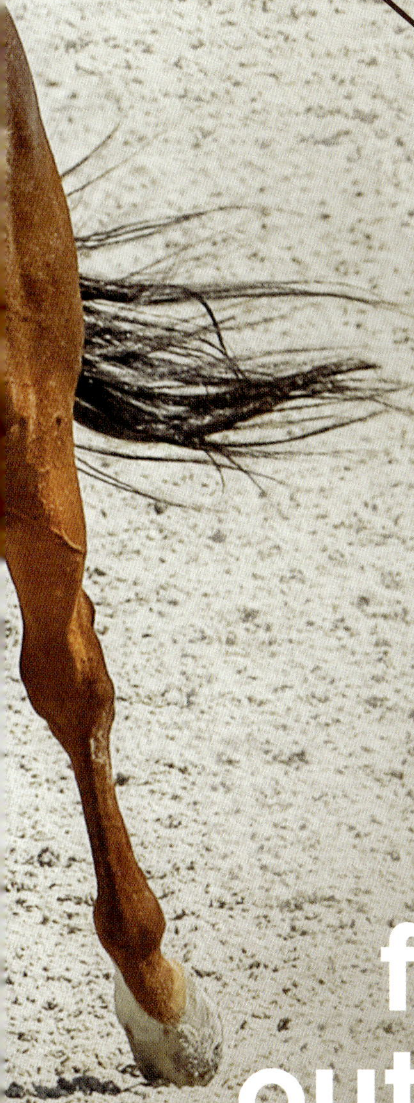

6

chapter

'd like to start this chapter with a statement that may surprise you. *You have two brains*. I know it's weird, but it's true! Your main brain is the one you see on the poster in science class and is a great brain to ride with because it has a calm-down center, memory center, goal-setting center, and many other centers that make riding successful and satisfying. Your secondary brain (called your "amygdala") doesn't have a calm-down center, memory center, or goal-setting center, it simply does five things. It makes you *fight, flight, freeze, freak out*, and *forget*!

You're going to act and react very differently to situations that make you feel either safe or stressful. You'll act calm and confident when feeling safe, and tight and tense when feeling stressed. Your reactions to these situ-

I wish you'd relax, Dottie. I don't know why you worry so much.

What makes you think I'm worried?

©ABERNETHY 2011

ations are rarely conscious, your brain simply interprets your emotions and automatically directs your behavior in the manner it feels most appropriate. When you're calm and confident, your main brain (most specifically your cerebral cortex) takes control and allows you to think clearly, make rational decisions, and recall things you'd like to remember. When you're nervous and stressed (feeling threatened) your amygdala takes control and keeps you safe by activating your fight-or-flight response.

You'll continue to act and react in appropriate ways to safe and stressful situations as long as your two brains play well together. Unfortunately, this isn't always the case. Sometimes the amygdala can get a bit greedy and take control of situations that aren't actually threatening. As a result, it's not uncommon for you to sometimes feel tight and tense when it would be bet-ter to remain calm and confident. This is called *amygdala hijack,* and I'll talk more about it later. For now, however, let's take a closer look at how your two different brains respond to stress.

Your amygdala, or what's often referred to as your "lizard brain," is an almond-shaped collection of cells in a region called the limbic system. Its main job is to 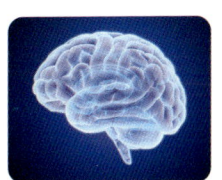 control the fear circuitry of your brain and is, therefore, responsible for firing the fight-or-flight response when it perceives a threat. That threat can be either *self-created* (like a fear of 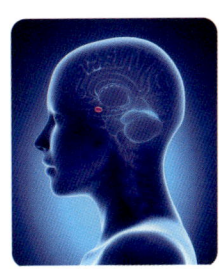 failure) or *situation-created* like running away from an enemy trying to harm you. The job of the amygdala is

129

*Challenges should make
you use your mind,
not lose your mind.*

Snake or
a stick?
Why don't
you ask your
lizard brain?

simple: create an automatic response to danger so you can *act without thinking* (it would rather you treat a stick like a snake than a snake like a stick).

Your amygdala activates the fight-or-flight response by sending a sort of distress signal to a part of your brain called the *hypothalamus*. Once received, it sends a signal to release the stress hormone *cortisol* and *adrenaline* into your bloodstream. Together, they work to increase your blood pressure, heart rate, respiration rate, and a few other things that provide your body with the quick burst of energy needed to fight or flee against the threat.

Your main brain, on the other hand, is responsible for rational thinking, decision-making, and planning. It's what allows you to process and think about your emotions so you can determine the most logical response to a situation. Unlike your lizard brain, however, your main brain

gives you *conscious* control over your responses so you can *think before acting* (to treat that stick like a stick rather than like a snake).

Ideally, the amygdala would interpret self-created threats (like a fear of riding in front of crowds) and situation-created threats (like a fear of harm) differently, but, unfortunately, it treats most threats the same. It simply feels that if you're feeling nervous you must be facing a threat. This means there's a good chance you'll react the same way to a fear of crowds as you do to a fear of harm. When this happens, your amygdala simply overreacts to the self-created threats and treats them as if you're facing a real threat that can harm you. Your main brain has now been hijacked.

●●● The Amygdala Hijack

Every time you experience a threat (either *self-* or *situation*-created), a part of your brain called the *thalamus* receives the threatening infor-

FIGHT, FLIGHT, AND...FREEZE?

Running away from a threat and fighting against it are understandable survival mechanisms, but how does freezing make any sense?

Well, freezing is camouflage. Many predators search out prey by movement, so some animals simply freeze as a way of hiding. Apparently movement is a dead giveaway (excuse the pun). Tell that to fainting goats! ●

Fergus BY JEAN ABERNETHY

Grace, what do people mean by "rational thought"?

Oh, that's just a little mind game they use to make decisions. It doesn't work very well, though.

For example, why do they put us on this side of the fence when all the good grass is over there?

TRUE STORY
(WELL...MAYBE NOT)

The world's smartest man, a famous doctor, a young boy, and an old man are in a plane that's about to crash, but they only have three parachutes. The world's smartest man grabs a chute and jumps saying he deserves to live because he's so intelligent, followed by the doctor who grabs a chute and jumps saying he deserves to live because he can save people. The old man grabs a chute, but gives it to the young boy instead and says, "I've lived a good life. You deserve the last chute." The young boy responds by saying, "Thank you, but we can both jump to safety—the world's smartest man just jumped out of the plane with my backpack!" ●

★ MORAL OF THE STORY:

The amygdala hijack makes it hard for rational people to do rational things!

mation and sends a signal to both your amygdala and main brain. Since survival is always given priority, the amygdala tends to receive the threat first, which allows it to activate the fight-or-flight response before your main brain has the time to determine if it's really the most logical choice.

Unfortunately, when this happens the amygdala disables the main brain (specifically the cerebral cortex), making it nearly impossible for you to think clearly, make rational decisions, stay calm, or control your thoughts and feelings. All of this occurs so quickly you're usually unaware it's even happening. The wiring of the amygdala's survival mechanism is so effective that you simply react before your main brain's thinking center has the chance to process what's really happening. Your main brain and all it's thinking, remembering, and calming centers have now been hijacked.

Your brain treats most threats equally, regardless if they come from a fear of failure or a real fear like the fear of being attacked by

a polar bear! Your amygdala convinces you that remaining calm and thinking rationally is wrong (the last thing you'd want to do when being attacked by a polar bear is calm down and try to remember what you did the last time you were being attacked by a polar bear!) What your amygdala really wants you to do is just tense up and prepare to fight or flee. The only problem is, overcoming self-created fears like a fear of failure requires calm and rational thinking! This is why it's sometimes so difficult (or

THE AMYGDALA HIJACK: CONNECTING THE DOTS

1. Your thalamus perceives you're nervous. ●

2. It assumes you're facing a threat (why else would you be nervous?). ●

3. It sends a distress signal to your main brain and amygdala. ●

4. Your amygdala receives the message first and engages the fight, flight, and freeze response before your main brain can determine if it's even a real threat. ●

5. You find it hard to think, remember, and calm down because your amygdala has shut off the parts of your main brain that controls them. ●

6. You've officially been hijacked, which is a big shame because the only threat you're really facing is riding in front of a judge (where thinking, remembering, and calming down would be best!). Unfortunately, your amygdala mistakenly treated your nervousness as a threat against your safety. It treated that stick like a snake! ●

Fergus BY JEAN ABERNETHY

When Fergus gets nervous I like to distract him with comical thoughts.

Remember that hilarious fainting goat we saw yesterday, Fergus?

Fergus?...

...it takes his mind off his anxiety.

even impossible) to relax and make quick decisions when you're feeling nervous. And why it's so important to learn how to overcome the *amygdala hijack.*

Stopping the Amygdala Hijack

Your hypothalamus and amygdala work together to create the fight-or-flight response by activating something called your *sympathetic nervous system.* This system works like a gas pedal, speeding up your heart and respiration rates in response to a self-created or real threat (it also creates other *psychosomatic symptoms* of stress like sweaty palms and shaking).

The opposite of the sympathetic nervous system is the *parasympathetic nervous system* that acts more like a brake, slowing your heart and respiration rate, so you can calm down and think rationally. The trick to stopping the amygdala hijack is, therefore, learning how to use your *parasympathetic brakes* at times when your sympathetic gas pedal is stuck to the floor!

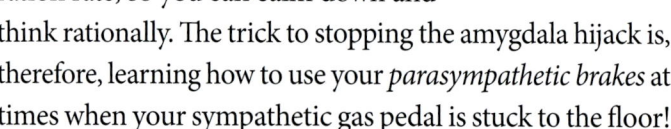

Another way to put the brakes on nervousness is to identify what triggers it. The next time you feel yourself getting tense and tight, pause for a moment, take a deep breath, and try to identify what's causing the anxiety. Is it *wondering* why you're so nervous, *worrying* you might lose, or *wishing* you weren't going first in a class? Once you identify the cause, simply label it as *mild* so your main brain can override your amygdala and allow you to calm down. You can also try reminding yourself that what you're feeling isn't really a real threat, it's just you overreacting to the fight-or-flight response trying to keep you safe.

● SPANKY not FRANKY!

When pumping your *parasympathetic brakes* doesn't quite do the trick, you're going to have to get a little creative.

THE 3-3-3-3 TRICK

The *amygdala hijack* makes it difficult to calm down and slow down, so the next time you're feeling nervous, give The 3-3-3-3 Trick a try. Take three deep breaths, name three things you see, three sounds you hear, then move three parts of your body. This is a great way of applying the brakes at a time when the gas pedal is stuck on the floor. ●

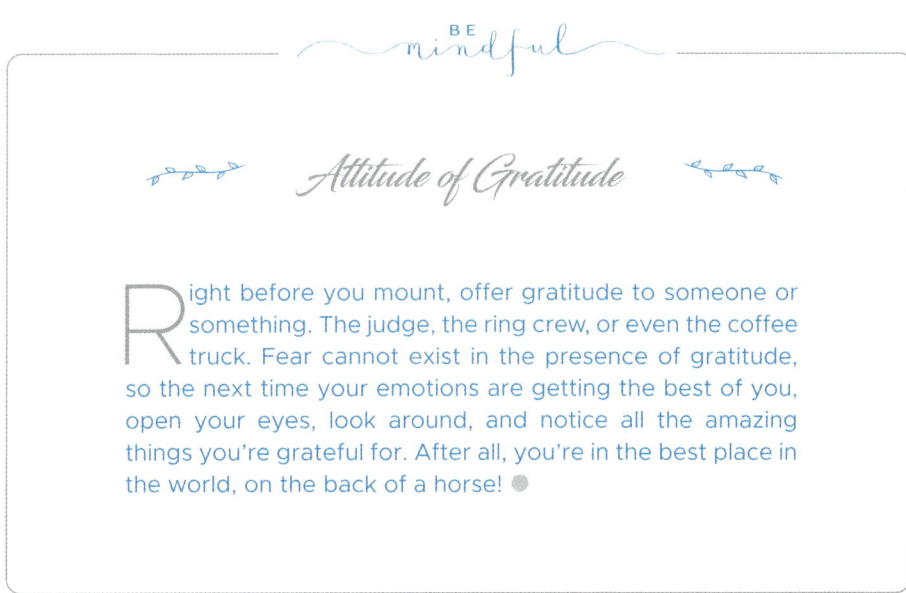

BE *mindful*

Attitude of Gratitude

Right before you mount, offer gratitude to someone or something. The judge, the ring crew, or even the coffee truck. Fear cannot exist in the presence of gratitude, so the next time your emotions are getting the best of you, open your eyes, look around, and notice all the amazing things you're grateful for. After all, you're in the best place in the world, on the back of a horse! ●

135

One way to do this is to *fake it till you make it.* In other words, when you want to feel confident, just act confident! You can do this by remembering the acronym SPANKY. The six calming tricks and techniques that make up this somewhat humorous acronym are guaranteed to help remove your foot from the gas pedal and place it on the brake. Let's look at the six tricks and techniques that make up SPANKY—one at a time:

SMILE

POWER POSTURE

ADRENALINE BREATH

NAME IT

KIND

YOUTHFUL

1. **S**MILE—When you're nervous you don't smile (you don't smile when being chased by a polar bear!). So if you're smiling, you're not nervous. That's the message you're sending to your brain. So the next time you feel anxious, give yourself

3 BREATHING TECHNIQUES

JUST breathe

You hold your breath when you're nervous, so the next time you get nervous... just breathe! Here are three easy breathing techniques to help apply the brakes to any runaway emotion:

1. Ratio Breathing: Breathe in for three seconds, hold it for two, and exhale for six (3 - 2 - 6 ratio). ●

2. Box Breathing: Inhale and exhale for four seconds each, but as you inhale, visualize drawing the upward line of a box, and as you exhale, visualize drawing the horizontal top line of that box. Now, exhale as you visualize drawing the dropping line of the box, and inhale while drawing the bottom horizontal line. When you're done, you'll have taken four deep breaths and drawn an entire box. Draw a few more if you like! ●

3. Pranayama Breathing: Inhale a full breath through your nose while sitting or standing tall. Hold your breath for two seconds and then constrict a portion of your breath (at the back of your throat) as you exhale slowly through your nose. If you're doing it right, it'll sound like a calming ocean wave or gentle rush of air. Repeat these soothing breaths for two minutes (longer if you can). ●

a little smile. It doesn't have be a big one, just turning-up the edges of your lips (called a half-smile) will release the *feel-good* hormones dopamine and serotonin, which work together to apply the *parasympathetic brakes* so you can calm down. When you smile you tell your brain you're not nervous (because you don't smile when you're nervous), so if you're smiling, you're not nervous, and if you're not nervous your amygdala won't hijack your main brain and its calm-down and memory centers!

2. POWER POSTURE— When you get nervous you get small. You drop your shoulders into the fetal position and do something called a "body-cross" (instinctively crossing your arms over your torso to protect your internal organs). So the next time

137

you get a little nervousness (at a time you'd normally get small) stand up extra tall, throw open your shoulders, and expand your chest (think standing like Superman or Wonder Woman). When you open yourself up into this kind of *alpha pose*, you tell your brain you're not nervous (because you don't go big when you're nervous). So if you're standing tall, you're not nervous, and if you're not nervous, your amygdala won't hijack your main brain and its calm-down and memory centers.

3. ADRENALINE BREATH—When you get nervous you instinctually hold your breath so you can engage your core muscles and recruit additional strength. It's a survival instinct caused by adrenaline and cortisol that increases your body's strength so you can fight or flee. So, the next time you get nervous, just breathe! The good news is that a few deep breaths is all you'll need to start removing the adrenaline and cortisol from your system so you can stop the *amygdala hijack*. When you're not nervous, your amygdala won't hijack your main brain and its calm-down and memory centers!

> Name it to tame it: Replacing the word nervous with excited is a simple way to make any situation feel better.

4. NAME IT—Being nervous and being excited are basically the same thing (adrenaline hits your system as you prepare for action), but the reason so many riders get nervous is simply because they tell themselves they're nervous. When you think those words, your amygdala hears them, perceives a threat, and hijacks your confidence. So the next time you feel the word *nervous* trying to come out, take a deep breath and change it to

the word *excited* (that warm-up arena doesn't make you nervous, it makes you excited). The good news is that you can't be nervous and excited at the same time, so if you're excited, you're not nervous, and if you're not nervous your amygdala won't hijack your main brain and its calm-down and memory centers!

5. <u>K</u>IND—When you get nervous you also tend to get a bit cranky. This means that if you can just stop the *cranky,* you can also stop much of the nervousness. One of the best ways to stop the cranky and feel better about yourself is to simply make an effort to do *kind* things to others. Even a quick act of kindness (called a five-second favor) like complimenting a competitor or thanking a volunteer can be enough to put the brakes on the *amygdala hijack.* Your brain simply believes that if you're feeling good enough to be kind to others, you mustn't be feeling very nervous, and if you're not feeling nervous, your amygdala won't hijack your main brain and its calm-down and memory centers!

6. <u>Y</u>OUTHFUL—Laughter is one of the strongest coping mechanisms against anxiety, but as you get older you begin to lose much of that laughter (most children laugh an average of 400 times a day, but adults only laugh an average of 17!). So the next time you begin to feel a bit nervous, take a deep breath and remind yourself how it felt to laugh and giggle and take things a little less seriously when you were a kid. Riding is a serious sport, but you should take your joy every bit as seriously as the rest of it! When you laugh, you tell your brain you're not nervous (because you don't laugh when you're nervous), so when you're laughing you're not nervous, and when

WIKIPEDIA SAYS:

Neoteny

DEAR BRAIN, I CAN'T ADULT TODAY

Retention of juvenile characteristics in adults, including a delight in learning experiences, along with curiosity and confidence without worrying what other people think.

Be silly. Be honest. Be kind.

- RALPH WALDO EMERSON -
Essayist and Poet

> Too blessed
> to be
> stressed.

you're not nervous, your amygdala won't hijack your main brain and its calm-down and memory centers!

The SPANKY acronym and its six confidence-building tricks can help you relax and regain your confidence because they encourage you to act in a way that's *opposite* of how you'd normally act when you're nervous (when you're not acting in a nervous way, your brain doesn't think you're nervous). This is the essence of *fake it till you make it* and is a wonderfully effective way to break the anxiety cycle mentioned in the last chapter (p. 103) and the *amygdala* hijack discussed in this one.

So the next time you're feeling *FRANKY* (frustrated and cranky) and can't think of a way to stop it, just think SPANKY! Whenever you feel frustrated because of a mistake, or cranky because your horse is misbehaving, take a deep breath, smile, open your shoulders, tell yourself you're excited, be kind to others, and laugh like you did when you were a kid! After all, that's the kind of riding life you deserve to live—one filled with confidence, courage, kindness, and kid-like exuberance!

141

●●● Memories

Your *amygdala* doesn't just control the fight, flight, or freeze response, it also controls what memories you store, what emotions are associated with those memories, and how strong those emotions will be. In other words, your amyg-  dala doesn't just control your moods; it controls your memories, too! When you're in a good mood (SPANKY) you tend to notice positive things and recall positive memories, and when you're in a bad mood (FRANKY) you tend to notice negative things and recall negative memories. This is called *mood-dependent retrieval* and it's great when you're in a good mood, but not so great when you're in a bad one.

●● Mood-Dependent Memories

The memories you experience are influenced by your mood. Not only are you more likely to recall good memories when you're in a good mood, but what you learned when you were happy is easier to recall when you're happy again. What you learned when you were unhappy is easier to recall when you're unhappy again. As a result, working to become a more positive and empowered rider (to be happy in your happy place) is one of the more important things you can do to ensure you'll become *bolder*, *braver*, and *brighter*.

If you're like most people, you might think memory is a bit like a filing cabinet with lots of files and folders, but it

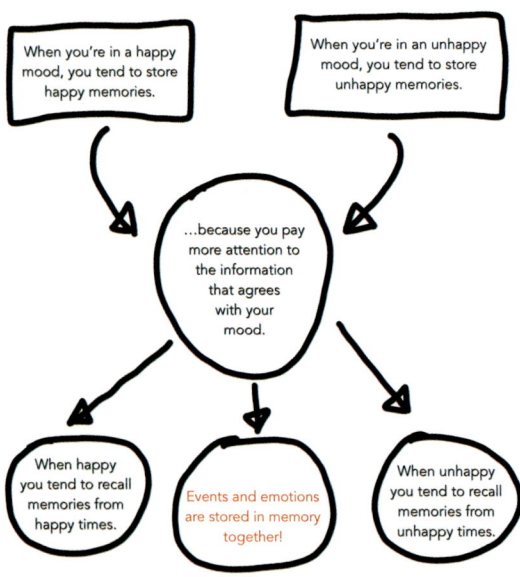

doesn't always work that way. In fact, many memories are actually created through *association*. For example, if you fell at a show last year, the next time you think of that show you might also think of the fall. These are called *associative memories*—when you think of one, you think of the other. In this way, memories work less like a filing cabinet and more like a knee-jerk reflex. When you think of one, you have a reflex to think of the other. You can also think of associative memories like *neuroplasticity* (ch. 5, p. 102), but instead of *neurons* being wired together and fired together, your *memories* are wired and fired together.

●● Short- and Long-Term Memories

You probably already know a lot about *short-* and *long-term memories*. (If not, please read my last three books!) Short-term memories typically last less than 30 seconds (it's actually helping you right now by storing information about the beginning of this sentence so you can make sense of the end of it), and it plays an important role in riding and problem-solving. For example, short-term memory is what allows you to make a mistake jumping Fence Number 1, but then avoid that same mistake when you jump Fence Number 2.

Long-term memories, on the other hand, can last from days to years. If you remember some-

FLASHBULB MEMORIES

Flashbulb memories are highly detailed *snapshots* of situations that you recall with amazing clarity. They're always related to an event, but are *autobiographical* in nature, meaning they always focus on you rather than the event. Remembering how you felt when you learned a good friend had fallen and gotten injured is an example of a flashbulb memory.●

143

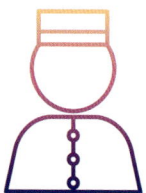

thing you did recently (whether it occurred yesterday or a decade ago) then it's a long-term memory. As with all memory, your mood influences the long-term memories you'll remember. Being in a good mood encourages the retrieval of good long-term memories. Being in a bad mood encourages the retrieval of bad ones.

Unfortunately, anxiety has a negative effect on short- and long-term memory because your amygdala gives priority to memories associated with threats and also shuts down the memory center in your main brain (remember, your amygdala doesn't think you need to remember what you did the last time you were being chased by a polar bear!). During times of stress, your amygdala works like a doorman. It lets some memories in (usually the bad ones) while keeping others out (usually the good ones). This is why it's so hard to remember good things when bad things happen to you.

There are two kinds of long-term memory, and each play an important role in riding. *Implicit* memories are those that don't require any effort to recall, and *explicit* memories are those that require conscious effort. While you can recite the days of the week without effort (implicit memory), it takes explicit memory to recall that you have an appointment with the farrier next Friday.

● Implicit Memory

This type of long-term memory is often referred to as *unconscious* memory because it happens without thinking. These memories use *associations* from your past that influence your thoughts and behaviors in the present. They help you recall the lyrics of your favorite song, ride

We all forget important things from time to time. Millions of trees are accidentally planted by squirrels who forget where they buried their nuts— proving that mistakes lead to growth!

a bike, and bridle your horse, but they also make it difficult to stop thinking about a fall last week or a disqualification last year. As with many things, implicit memory can be used for good or evil. There are two types of implicit memory:

1. **Procedural Memories**—These memories allow you to learn and perform physical skills (like trotting, cantering, and jumping) without thinking about it. Taking the same route to the barn every day and remembering how to bridle your horse are other examples of *procedural* memory.

2. **Priming Memories**—You can be *primed* to remember certain memories by increasing your exposure to them. For example, if you're asked to name an animal starting with "ho" you'll probably say horse…unless you have a howler monkey, horny toad, or honey bees at home.

Explicit Memories

Unlike implicit memories, it takes a conscious effort to retrieve things from your *explicit* memory. Memorizing a dressage test or naming the breeds of horses are examples of explicit memories. These memories are always influenced by your mood; the more anxious you are, the harder it is to remember them. There are two kinds of explicit memory:

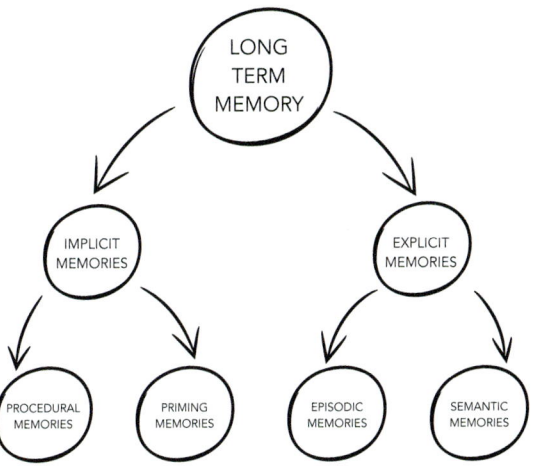

1. **Episodic Memories**—These memories are based on a combination of experiences and events (episodes). How well you remember episodes depends on several factors, including their outcomes. For example, it's easier to remember a memory if there was a *fall* or *fail* episode attached to it because your amygdala gives priority to those memories.

145

2. **Semantic Memories**—These are long-term memories that aren't created by experiences or events (episodes). Semantic memory includes things that are common knowledge like the names of colors, that zebras have stripes and a horse has a mane.

● ● ● The Problem with Memories

Memories can be used for *good* (remembering your jump course) and evil (when you can't stop thinking about forgetting your jump course). *Priming* and *episodic* memories tend to get you into most trouble. After all, it's not bad when anxiety makes you forget that zebras have stripes, but it is bad when an anxious episode makes you lose confidence in yourself.

There are two main problems with memories. First, they're tied to your emotions so anytime you feel anxious there's a good chance you'll recall anxious memories. Second, troubling memories often get *repressed* (pushed below the surface of your awareness) where you think they no longer exist. These are perhaps the most troubling memories of all. For example, you might not remember falling during a trail ride when you were six, but for some reason you're still afraid of riding in open spaces twenty years later. Unless you unlock (become mindful of) repressed memories like these, they'll be nearly impossible to overcome.

● ● Repressed Memories

Significant events in your life will linger in your memory. Some memories make you happy and others make you sad, but when your brain registers a memory that is too sad, it might drop it into a sort of *unconscious* zone where you don't have to think about it anymore. The real problem with repressing memories like this is that they might *feel* gone, but they're certainly not forgotten. They'll continue to operate below the surface of awareness, directing your behaviors in ways that might be difficult to understand (being afraid of something, but not knowing why). Unfortunately, when distressing memories are repressed, they get stuck in a place where you just can't solve or overcome them.

Memory repression is the unconscious defense mechanism that happens when your brain labels a memory as too distressing, but the same thing happens when you *purposely* repress distressing memories. This is called *suppression.* The only way to overcome repressed and suppressed memories is to bring them back to the surface of awareness where you can see them, understand them, and begin to overcome them. Unfortunately, when they remain hidden, they'll continue to have a negative impact on your thoughts and behaviors.

●●● Five Fixes for Troubling Memories

Since troubling memories are influenced by your moods, and easily repressed or suppressed, the best ways to solve them are to (1) learn to alter your mood (think SPANKY not FRANKY), and (2) bring any hidden memories back to the surface where you can address them. The following five tips can help you accomplish both:

1. **Use a Mood Modifier**—Since mood affects your memories, you can increase the likelihood of remembering positive memories by using a few positive mood-modifiers like smiling, laughing, and listening to uplifting

A bird is never afraid the branch will break because her trust is not in the branch, but in her ability to fly. Always trust your ability to fly.

music. They won't only help you recall more positive past memories, they'll also help you create more positive present memories that you can draw upon in the future.

2. **Phone a Friend**—Sometimes dealing with hidden memories can feel overwhelming so ask a trusted friend or family member if they can help you recall any re-pressed or suppressed memories. There's a good chance they might be hidden to you, but in plain sight to them. Allowing them to help you uncover these memories is a great way to end the *wondering, wishing*, and *worrying* that hidden memories might be causing you.

3. **Push Pause**—Help yourself overcome troubling mem-ories by image-watching them on TV. If they become too difficult, just push an imaginary *pause* button (or *fast-forward* button if you prefer to skip the hard-est parts). When you feel a bit better, hit rewind and imagine watching the video (your troubling memories) again—only this time, try and watch it a little longer before hitting the pause or the fast-forward button.

4. **Get Off the One-Off**—Distressing memories usually come from *one-off experiences* (those that rarely happen again, but you can't stop thinking about), so remind yourself that most of your troubling memories only come from something that happened in your past, and not likely to happen again in your future. If you can make this connection, you can take the power away from the memory.

5. **Look Back to Go Forward**—Your brain can only focus on one thing at a time (called *selective attention*) so the next time you're struggling with a distressing memory, try replacing it with a positive one. This is called *memory motivation*: using an empowering memory from your past to motivate you to become more positive in the present. The good news is that (as a rider) you're sure to have plenty of great memories to draw upon! ●

STRESS-INDUCED AMNESIA

Did you know there's a relationship between pressure and memory? When pressure goes up, your memory goes down! That's why you can never find your car keys when you're in a rush. It's also why you remember your dressage tests and jump courses easily on Wednesday after school or work (when no one's watching), but forget them at the show on Saturday when the judges are judging and people are watching. When pressure goes up, your memory goes down! ●

NEVER LET ANYTHING
THAT WILL ULTIMATELY
MEAN NOTHING KEEP
YOU FROM EXPERIENCING
SOMETHING THAT COULD
MEAN EVERYTHING.

7

chapter

have a little faith in failure

7

chapter

Failure gets a bad rap. You think you know what failure means and does, but in fact, there are a few things about it that might really surprise you, for example, the fact that you actually enjoy it, seek it, and are highly motivated by it. To help you understand (and believe) this, I'm beginning this chapter with my all-time favorite subject. It's called the *Subway Surfers Effect* and it proves that you enjoy failure, seek it out, and are very motivated by it.

●●● Subway Surfers Effect

Every time you play a game (like *Subway Surfers*) you're going to fail. You'll trip, get hit by a train, run into a barrier, or get caught by the policeman. But one thing's for sure, you're going to fail! If you're like most people, however, you don't quit and throw your device to the floor each time you fail, instead you hit the start button again so you can test what you just learned. You'll dodge left a little faster or jump the train a little earlier next time, and in doing so, prove that your past failures work to create better future outcomes.

Every time you hit that start button you'll fail again, and in doing so, learn a few new tricks you didn't know before. Every time you come back, you'll come back a little smarter and run a little faster, jump a little higher, and collect a few more coins. And when that happens, there'll be no denying that your past failures weren't setting you back, they were setting you up for improved success.

Playing a game like *Subway Surfers* proves that you're capable of focusing on achievements rather than failures. After all, you ask your friends, "What level did you achieve"  rather than, "How did you die?" The failing isn't the interesting part, it's what was achieved that piqued your interest. Instead of focusing on how you failed, you focus on how much farther you got, how many more coins you grabbed, or how many more points you scored. When it comes to the *Subway Surfers Effect*, you don't frame your failures as bad, you reframe them as good things that make you better.

But here's the real interesting part. If you never failed (meaning you never got hit by the train or caught by the policeman) you would probably never want to play the game again! After all, what's the fun in that? What's the fun in doing something so easy you never feel challenged or motivated? The real fun comes from overcoming the challenges, learning from them, and using them to help you improve. That's the reason so many people love these silly games. Because they fail!

If that wasn't enough, here's yet another positive message hidden in the *Subway Surfers Effect*. Imagine you're a developer hoping to create a new and exciting game like Candy Crush or PAC-MAN—a game that captures everyone's attention and makes you lots of money. Would you design your game so that it was void of challenges? Would you design it so the players would never fail? Well, if you did, you better start looking for a new career because no one would ever buy it! The true value in the game comes from the unending obstacles that motivate you to be better. Without them, the game just wouldn't be worth the money.

●●● Live Life Like a Game

When it comes to overcoming the stigma surrounding failure, perhaps all you need to do is imagine your life like a game. Embrace all the

> *Happiness can be found even in the darkest of times, if only you remember to turn on the light.*
>
> - HARRY POTTER AND THE PRISONER OF AZKABAN -
> by J.K. Rowling

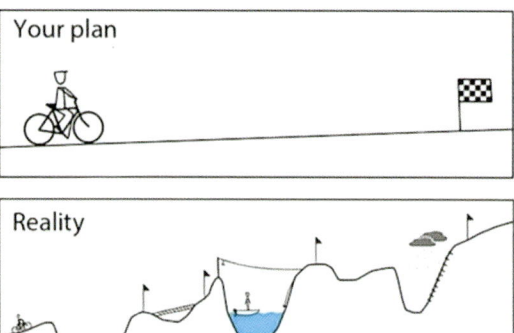

unexpected and valuable challenges and obstacles that riding provides. Having just a little faith in failure can break down the barriers standing between your obstacles and the lessons they're trying to teach you. While they might come in the form of forgotten courses or pulled rails instead of trains and policemen, the formula will always be the same. Past failures don't set you back, they set you up for future success.

●● Labeling

Before you can develop a faith in failure, you must first learn to take yourself out of the equation. Most riders who struggle with failure don't actually struggle with the failure itself, but with the false and defeating belief that they are *the failure,* using the word to define themselves rather than the situation. This is called *labeling* and is what causes so many riders to get mad at themselves, become pessimistic, and feel hopelessness. The first step in developing a faith in failure is to remember that it's not all about you!

It's very important to remember that failure is always an event, but never a person. It's just a thing that happened. You can be hard-working, talented, and resilient, and still fail from time to time. Labels like *failure* or *not good enough* are sticky and powerful so learn to avoid them when describing yourself. Sure you'll fail from time to time, but give yourself a break and come up with other more correct labels that define you. Hard-working, talented, and resilient are great examples because they don't define a thing that happened, but who you are.

The labels you attach to yourself are powerful. They either help or hinder your ability to feel valuable and satisfied, and are usually *self-prophetic,* meaning you

When you learned to walk and fell 50 times you never thought, "Maybe this isn't for me." Fall down 50 times; get up 51!

Fergus BY JEAN ABERNETHY

Fergus! Fergus! I have a question!

Yes?

If you try to fail, and succeed...

...which have you done?

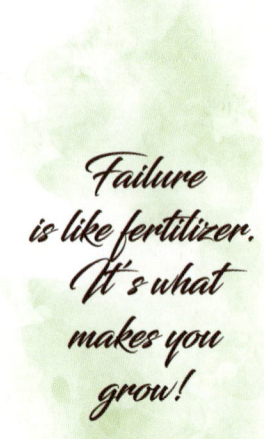

Failure is like fertilizer. It's what makes you grow!

become what you label yourself. If your labels are self-defeating and pessimistic, you'll form emotional barriers between you and your ability to feel valuable and satisfied. When your labels are encouraging and optimistic, however, these barriers come down. Whenever you create a label in your mind, you give it power, so make sure you point that power in the right direction!

●● Take Yourself Out of the Equation

One step in developing a faith in failure is to take yourself out of the equation. This is called *dissociation* because you no longer associate yourself with the failure. You simply cannot be defined by an event, mistake, or failure. Yes, you may have failed at something, but you're not *the* failure. Yes, you may have lost at something, but you are not a loser. A single moment in time cannot define who you are. Dissociation allows you to remove yourself from the failure so that you can label the event a failed attempt, rather than yourself a failed rider.

Stay upbeat, even when you're feeling beat-up.
You don't have to fall apart
just because things are falling apart!

Mindfulness is another key to developing a faith in failure. Becoming aware of the tendency to label yourself in a negative way is just as important as separating yourself from the failure itself. Stressful and meaningful events can sometimes cause you to blow things out of proportion (including the size of your shortcomings) so becoming mindful of those tendencies can help you remove yourself from the equation, and in doing so, see more clearly the lessons they're trying to teach you.

Self-talk also plays a role in developing a faith in failure. The words you say to yourself are also self-prophetic (be careful what you wish for, you might just get it). Learning to discuss failure as an event rather than a person (you) goes a long way to removing its power. Great riders fail all the time, and are given plenty of reasons to believe they could be failures, but they don't. Instead of saying, "I'm a failure," they say things like, "I missed that one," or "That was my bad," or "I'll get it next time." They focus on what they learned from the event and are excited to prove that they can fail forward the next time. Is it easy? No. Is it possible? Yes!

●●● Myths and Misconceptions about Messing Up

There are many misunderstandings about failure that can make it almost impossible to accept or overcome. When the myths and misconceptions go away, however, so do the problems they create.

The first misconception is that failure is avoidable. Some riders believe that if they can just get a little bit better they can avoid future failures. The only

> *We don't make mistakes,*
> *just happy little accidents.*

- BOB ROSS -
Painter and Television Host

Success is like
chocolate—
sometimes
there will be
a little bitter
before
the sweet.

problem with this theory is that you can always get a bit better, meaning you'll always find new challenges that'll lead to new forms of failure. It's not that you can't do them, it's just that you can't do them—*yet*. Everyone fails, but how much it hurts really depends on whether you believe it's avoidable or not. Give yourself permission to fail from time to time, and you give yourself the chance to have a little faith in the failure.

A second misconception is that failure is a single moment in time. In fact, failure is no more a single moment in time than is success. It's a process. You know success doesn't happen all at once. It takes years of hard work and determination. Success is a journey not a destination. Failure might feel like the end destination, but it was built upon the journey too. It's the culmination of the process. If you forget your dressage test, it's not because of that moment in time, it's because of the actions that led up to it. Change your actions next time (e.g. arrive earlier so you can visualize your test) and you can change the result. Your failures are some of your best teachers, as long as you're willing to believe it.

A third misconception is that failure is final. Stick a fork in it because you're done. In fact, failure isn't the end, it's the beginning! It's a stepping-off point from where you begin to find a way to solve past disappointments by altering your future behaviors. Failure might come in the form of a mess, but the *mess*age is clear: it's the *lessons learned* and *toughness earned* from failures that'll help you avoid making the same mistakes in the future.

One final misconception is that failure is bad! Many people believe failure is the enemy and try to avoid it at all costs. They think if they stay in their comfort zone and avoid all challenges, they'll become a success. But it doesn't work that way. Failure is good and avoidance is bad. No one ever learned a skill by avoiding it. Failure is learning and learning is good, therefore, failure is good!

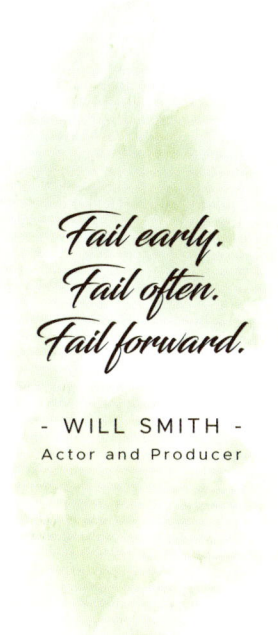

Fail early.
Fail often.
Fail forward.

- WILL SMITH -
Actor and Producer

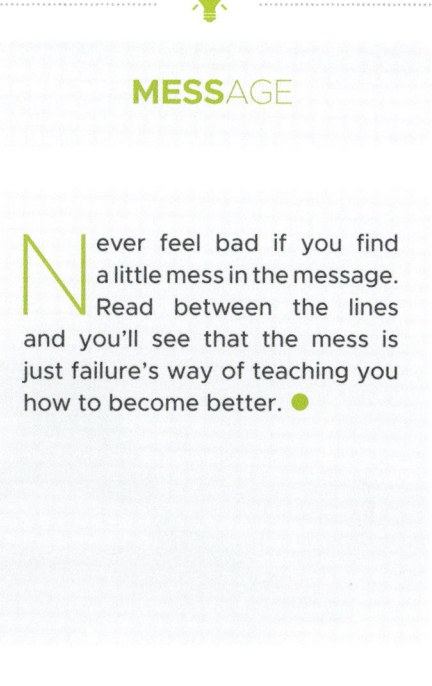

MESSAGE

Never feel bad if you find a little mess in the message. Read between the lines and you'll see that the mess is just failure's way of teaching you how to become better. ●

●●● Kinds of Failures

Your perception of failure influences how you react to it and recover from it. Resilient riders have the ability to avoid taking failure personally. They don't think they're worthless or let it affect their confidence. They simply see it as a temporary setback, a question that needs to be answered, or a pill that might not taste particularly good, but one that will make them better.

There are three main categories of failure, but only one should cause you any concern.

I think my silver lining is a bit tarnished.

1. *Complexity-Related Failure*—This category of failure is usually unavoidable because you're attempting a skill with a high degree of difficulty.

2. *Intelligent Failure*—This category is also unavoidable and usually provides the most information because it happens when you try something for the first time.

3. *Preventable Failure*—This is the category of failure that happens when you don't do what you know you should've done.

As you can imagine, preventable failure is the category most riders struggle with because it leads to regret (would've, could've, should've) so let's look more closely at it now. There are six kinds of preventable failure and I've listed them for you below. Perhaps becoming mindful of them will help you to jump out of the way before they hit you!

1. **Accomplishment**—*Accomplishment failure* happens when you attempt something but don't succeed. It can be a bit disheartening, and leave you wondering why you couldn't finish

161

EGO DEPLETION

What comes easy won't last, and what lasts won't come easy.

Sometimes motivation can feel like a limited resource. Like a muscle, it has strength but can be easily fatigued. Ego depletion happens when you give up because you feel you've used up all your motivation.

the job, but it does provide you with a record of what happened so you can build upon it next time. Forgetting your dressage test is a good example of accomplishment failure.

2. **Attention**—Some riders think they're a bit too good for their own good. As a result, they don't always listen to their trainers, which often results in uncharacteristic mistakes. They didn't fail because they can't do it; they failed

because they didn't pay attention. Falling on course because you didn't listen to your trainer's comments about the footing is a good example of *attention failure*.

3. **Motivation**—This kind of failure occurs when you don't finish what you start. It usually begins with a series of small mistakes that make you wish you could stop and start over. In the end, your motivation suffers and you make even more mistakes. Knocking over the last jump because the first one came down is a good example of *motivation failure*.

4. **Method**—Sometime you'll succeed, but still feel like you failed because it didn't happen the way you'd hoped. This kind of failure stings a bit less than the others because the outcome was what you'd hoped for, but the process of getting there wasn't. Winning a class because the other riders were disqualified (even though you rode poorly) is a good example of method failure.

5. **Recognition**—*Recognition failure* occurs when you fail to take into consideration how your actions affect others. Failing to arrive on time for a group lesson or continually forgetting to clean the wash-rack are considered *failure of recognition*. These failures are common amongst egocentric riders and can only be eliminated by developing a more mature sense of self.

Life always offers you a second chance. It's called tomorrow.

FIVE Ms
TO MASTERY

1. Misstep
I'm walking through the pasture. There's a big hole. I fall into it. My bad! ●

2. Missed Opportunity
I'm walking through the pasture. There's a big hole. I fall into it again. That's silly. I knew better. ●

3. Mistake
I'm walking through the pasture. There's a big hole. I know it's there but fall into it anyway. It's becoming a bad habit. This is my first mistake. ●

4. Mindfulness
I'm walking through the pasture. There's a big hole. I walk around it. ●

5. Mastery
I walk through another pasture. ●

Notice how a mistake wasn't really a mistake until you repeated it a few times!

6. Anticipation—Sometimes, you might fail to anticipate important things. You can't always predict, but you can prepare, which means *preparation* is the key to avoiding *anticipatory failure.* Your horse refusing a fence because you forgot to alter your approach after hearing the footing was bad, is a good example of anticipatory failure.

●●● Reframe the Picture

Developing the skill of owning, accepting, and learning from your failures isn't easy, but a technique called *reframing* can help. Reframing happens when you learn to view (reframe) your failures and mistakes in

> *Change the way you look at things and the things you look at change*

a positive way. For example, instead of viewing them as missed opportunities, you reframe them as learning opportunities. Regardless of the situation, you can reframe almost any negative event into a positive one. Like Einstein said, "In the middle of every difficulty lies an opportunity." You just need to believe it!

An important sub-skill of reframing is *curiosity*. Instead of wishing the mistake or failure didn't happen, you use curiosity and self-directed questions to seek out the cause (if you can find it, you can fix it!). Two-part questions like, "What caused me to get time faults, and how can I avoid them in the future?" or "What caused my last fence to come down, and how can I keep it up next time?" are examples of how curiosity and self-directed questions can lead to learning.

Reframing a failure into something more positive is a four-part puzzle.

When all the pieces come together, they help change what the failure means and how you feel about it. The four puzzle pieces of the reframing puzzle are *accept, acquire, advance*, and *achieve*.

YOU TURNED RIGHT BUT IT STILL WENT WRONG!

The next time you fail, learn to improve your future performances by asking yourself these three questions:

1. Was the failure caused by unrealistic expectations? ●

2. What successes were hidden in the failure? ●

3. What am I grateful for (what did I learn)? ●

- **Accept:** Yup, it's your fault. Your 100 percent wasn't enough. Many riders will try to blame it on the wind, the judge, or their horse. But not you. You'll *accept* responsibility for it so you can get on with fixing it.

- **Acquire:** You've admitted and accepted it. Your curiosity and self-directed questions can now help you *acquire* the message the failure was trying to teach you all along. You can now get on with learning.

DARE GREATLY

Our twenty-sixth president, Theodore Roosevelt, famously said: "It is not the critic who counts; not the man who points out how the strong man stumbles, or where the doer of deeds could have done them better. The credit belongs to the man who is actually in the arena, whose face is marred by dust and sweat and blood; who strives valiantly; who errs, who comes short again and again, because there is no effort without error and shortcoming; but who does actually strive to do the deeds; who knows great enthusiasms, the great devotions; who spends himself in a worthy cause; who at the best knows in the end the triumph of high achievement, and who at the worst, if he fails, at least fails while daring greatly, so that his place shall never be with those cold and timid souls who neither know victory nor defeat." ●

● **Advance:** You've accepted and acquired the knowledge needed to fix the failure. Many riders are still trying to ignore or blame the mistake away, but not you. You can now *advance* and get on with moving on!

● **Achieve:** You've accepted, acquired, and advanced. Some riders are still looking for excuses, but not you. You've now *achieved* the ability to do that thing you couldn't do before!

●●● Eight Fixes for Failure

It's been said that struggle builds strength. Luckily, failure is the perfect vehicle for delivering that struggle! There'll be no shortage of mistakes and failures in your future, and thankfully there is also no shortage of things you can do to overcome them. Here are eight techniques that can help you find a little faith in failure.

1. **Experiment**—Call your failures *experiments*. After all, you're testing things out and learning from them. Sure some of them might catch fire or explode, but you'll definitely learn something from them that you didn't know before (and they'll help make all your future experiments less threatening).

2. **Improve, Don't Prove**—Always set goals that'll improve your skills and behaviors, not *prove* yourself to others. Failing is a part of both. Failure will help improve your

SCIENTIFIC METHOD

The scientific method depends on trial and error. If the results confirm the hypothesis, it's called a "measurement." If it fails, it's called a "discovery." Failure is about discovery. •

skills and behaviors, but when trying to impress others, failure will hurt your sense of self and possibly create a fear of future failure.

3. **Give Credit Where Credit Is Due**—Always remember that your success (or lack of it) is never someone else's responsibility. When you come up short, attribute it to something you did or didn't do. Instead of saying, "The judge is mean," take credit by saying something like, "I could've made better choices today, and will be sure to do so in the future."

4. **Give Yourself a Quota**—Separating your expectations from perfection makes failures feel less threatening. One way to do this is to give yourself a *failure quota*—a set number of mistakes per ride, lesson, or show. Start with a quota of three or four, but add or subtract a few if the skill is particularly easy or hard.

5. **Take Some Time**—The more disappointing your disappointments are, the more time you'll need to get over them. Instead of expecting to immediately bounce back, give yourself a *time quota*. For example, allow yourself to feel bad about it

You have the right to be wrong sometimes.

167

TRUE STORY

Meaningful messages about failure can be found in the strangest places. I read an article once where researchers attempted to study the intelligence of sea animals by placing a Spanish mackerel in the same tank as a barracuda (its natural predator). Luckily for the mackerel, there was a piece of glass separating the two fish, so when the barracuda attacked, it just bonked its nose on the unseen barrier. Undeterred, the barracuda continued to attack, but the results were always the same. Before long, the barracuda lost interest (or was suffering from a really sore nose) and gave up.

Sometime later, the researchers removed the barrier from the tank. Now, even though there was nothing separating the two fish, the barracuda showed no interest in trying to eat the mackerel. It had given up. It had suffered too many failures and grew too tired of trying and never succeeding. These two fish lived in this barrier-free tank for over two years, and all the barracuda had to do during this time, was try one more time.

Riders often allow failures to place a barrier between them and their goals. They keep making mistakes and at some point grow tired of trying and failing. They hit the wall so many times they quit, even though all they need to do is just try one more time. ●

★ MORAL OF THE STORY:

Never allow failure to build a barrier between you and your goals. When it happens, just try one more time and have a little faith in failure!

until tomorrow morning. After that, take a deep breath and move on.

6. **Practice for Failure**—You get better at everything you practice, so get better at failing by *practicing failure*. Most riders practice for success (by doing what you're good at) but that doesn't help strengthen your failure tolerance. Push yourself outside your comfort zone during your lessons and be okay with what you find out there (spoiler alert: it will be frequent failure).

Practice failures and you can fail your way to success.

7. **Pencil in Your Goals**—Reduce the sting of failure by writing your goals in *pencil* instead of pen. Even if you fail to achieve one, you can erase it and set a new one based on what you just learned. Most riders only want the warm fuzzy feeling of achieving goals, but the cold prickly feelings are just as helpful!

8. **Create Contentment**—Our culture doesn't always encourage contentment. We constantly want a bigger house and fancier horse. Social media makes you want longer legs and whiter teeth. Teach yourself to be content with learning, even if it's through failure. ●

EVEN THE MOST SUCCESSFUL PEOPLE FAIL

1. **Walt Disney** *was once fired from a newspaper because of a lack of creativity.* ●

2. **Steve Jobs** *was fired from Apple.* ●

3. **Michael Jordan** *was cut from his high school basketball team.* ●

4. **Thomas Edison** *was fired from his first two jobs because he wasn't productive enough.* ●

5. **Henry Ford** *is famous for building the Model T, because models A through S failed!* ●

6. **J.K. Rowling** *was rejected 12 times before someone agreed to publish her Harry Potter books.* ●

7. **Oprah** *was considered unfit for television by a TV producer.* ●

169

8

chapter

your ego is not
your amigo

8

chapter

Being brave requires an understanding that there's always going to be a hard way and an easy way, but that the easy way is rarely the right way. Tough sports like riding require tough decisions made by equally tough athletes. However, these decisions just don't happen when you're always looking for an easy way out, blaming disappointing outcomes on others, or avoiding challenges altogether. Courage only comes from making effort and errors, getting up after you've fallen (mentally or physically), and taking on challenges when it would be easier to take a pass.

Don't wait for all the lights to be green before you leave the house.

Riding gives you the opportunity to build your bravery on an almost daily basis. Some of these opportunities come in the form of good challenges (like learning to jump), and others come in the form of bad luck (like falling while learning to jump!). Since many of these challenges might lead you to question your courage, it's always a good idea to have a few strategies to help you cope with the many emotions that might arise. The strategies are called *coping mechanisms*—a combination of purposeful thoughts and behaviors that help you cope, accept, and overcome difficulties and disappointments.

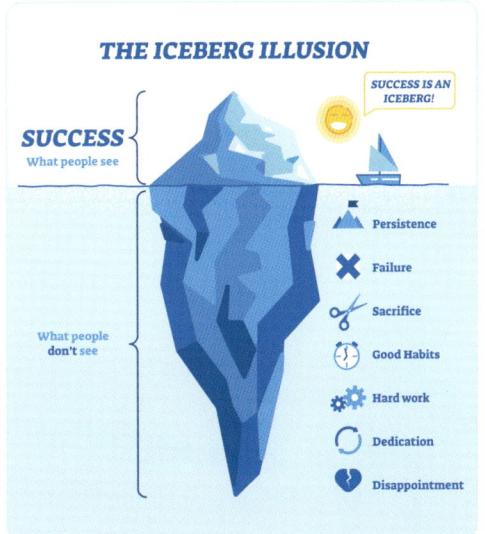

●●● Coping Mechanisms vs. Defense Mechanisms

> You often don't see all that leads to someone's success.

It's common for these two terms to be used interchangeably, but they're actually very different. While they share some similarities, they function in very different ways.

Coping mechanisms (also called *adaptive strategies*) are empowering strategies that remove negative thoughts and resolve stressful events in a positive way. *Defense mechanisms*, on the other hand, are protective strategies (called *maladaptive strategies*) that protect fragile egos from accepting responsibility for mistakes and failures by doing things like blaming them on others or saying they never happened. For this

TWO WAYS TO HANDLE STRESSFUL SITUATIONS

1. **Emotionally Focused Response:** positive coping strategies (like meditation, mindfulness, and relaxation techniques) that help you manage stressful situations. ●

2. **Appraisal Focused Response:** negative coping strategies (like denial, blaming, and avoidance) that make stressful situations appear less personal. ●

reason, defense mechanisms are also called *ego defenses* because their only goal is to protect the fragile ego of the person.

Coping mechanisms are purposeful and empowering mental strategies used to lessen the impact of stressful events and prevent them from feeling overwhelming. When used correctly, they help you feel in control of your emotions instead of feeling like your emotions are controlling you.

Defense mechanisms, on the other hand, are unconscious negative thoughts and behaviors that occur when you feel incapable of *coping* with stressful thoughts or events. Unfortunately, they can distort reality because they might make you feel like the troubling situation has gone away when in fact it hasn't. *Ego defenses* may make you feel momentarily detached from the problem, but they certainly don't help you to solve it.

●● Defense Mechanisms

A fragile ego can get you into a lot of trouble. It's what causes you to blame your mistakes on others, repress troubling emotions instead of sharing them with your trainer, and avoid

Things turn out best when you make the best of the way things turn out.

Fergus BY Jean Abernethy

Look at that! She's scared of her own shadow!

Yup, packin' panic, I'd say. Zero stress management techniques.

In theory, her anxiety could be the result of a chemical imbalance.

She may have a lower-than-normal level of neuro-transmitters in her brain.

Wow! You've really studied up on equine biochemistry.

I was referring to the rider.

taking responsibility for upsetting outcomes. It's also a major cause of fear of failure and perfectionism. So, it goes without saying that your ego is definitely not always your amigo!

There are many different kinds of *defense mechanisms.* The six most common are listed below. As you'll see, most consist of some form of excuse-making, avoidance, or denial that give you the impression the problem is gone (but unfortunately, not forgotten). Listed below them are six *positive coping mechanisms.* Instead of excuse-making, avoidance, and denial, they consist of strategies that help you accept and resolve problems. Gone and forgotten!

● { **1** } Denial

Denial occurs when you refuse to accept responsibility for your mistakes and mess-ups. Instead of admitting and owning them (so you can learn from them) you block them from your mind so you don't have to deal with them. In other words, you deny responsibility for the bad things so you can avoid the bad feelings that accompany them. A rider who denies responsibility for a poor dressage score (even though she knows she rode poorly), or a rider who forgets her course but refuses to admit she could've done better (by visualizing it before starting), are examples of denial. Unfortunately, denial can get you into a lot of trouble because you can't disregard reality and get away with it for long.

● { **2** } Projection

Projection happens when you place unwanted thoughts or feelings onto someone else, or when you react to your own unacceptable impulses as though they were happening to someone else. In this way, you *project* your unacceptable feelings onto others so you can avoid the guilt and shame of feeling them yourself. Two examples of projection would be (1) worrying about a judge, but making yourself feel better by saying she dislikes you, and (2) saying something like, "I'm not the one who's afraid of failure, you're the one who's the perfectionist!" As you can see, projection is usually used to protect your ego by projecting bad things onto good people.

I'm not in denial—I'm just selective about the reality I accept.

● { **3** } Repression

Upsetting thoughts and memories can sometimes leave you feeling a bit self-conscious and emotionally vulnerable. *Repression* happens when you try to hide (repress) those feelings (instead of facing them) in hopes of feeling better about yourself. An example of repression you might hear at a horse show would sound something like, "I don't know what you're talking

> Confidence
> is like
> a camera.
> Focus on
> what's
> important,
> capture the
> good times,
> develop from
> the negatives,
> and if things
> don't work
> out, take
> another shot!

about, I never get nervous riding in front of crowds!" (even though she does!), or when an entry-level rider says a little too enthusiastically, "Of course I know my diagonals!" even though she has no idea what you're talking about. Unfortunately, your brain knows when you're lying to yourself, so repression usually just creates additional feelings of disappointment.

● { **4** } Displacement

Displacement doesn't happen when you deny, project, or repress disappointing or frustrating thoughts and behaviors, it happens when you direct them toward something else. Throwing a baseball bat to the ground or breaking a tennis racket are common examples of how athletes use *displacement* to satisfy a negative impulse without suffering significant consequences. Our sport, however, is not nearly as forgiving. While throwing your gloves to the ground after a disappointing round won't help or hurt, tak-

ing your frustration out on your horse with a smack or a yank is always unacceptable. Riders who have an ego large enough to allow them to do this should really ask themselves if riding is the right sport for them….

● { **5** } Rationalization

Rationalization happens when you invent logical reasons why bad things happen, distort *the facts* so you can make disappointing situations feel less disappointing, or create

FOCUS ON
MOTIVATION ON
DEDICATION ON
EXCUSES OFF

your own set of facts to convince yourself that everything's okay (even though it's not). Most people use rationalization to justify poor outcomes so that they can feel better about their bad behaviors, but rationalization simply comes down to making excuses. "I knew I was going to forget my dressage test because I've had bad cramps and a headache all day," is a good example of rationalization. Forgetting the test can leave you a bit emotionally wounded, so blaming it on a rational reason like cramps and a headache protects your ego from having to accept that it was your fault.

● { 6 } Avoidance

When a situation creates too much anxiety, one convenient option is simply to *avoid* it altogether. Although some people (especially those with fragile egos) might think this is an acceptable way to cope with challenges, refusing to confront them only makes them feel bigger and more overwhelming. A rider with a fear of crowds, for example, is engaging in avoidance when she refuses to ride in group lessons, take clinics, or compete at local shows. While she feels this strategy might solve the problem, it only adds shame to the avoidance that makes the small problem feel bigger. The only way to overcome avoidance is simply to summon the courage and *do it afraid*.

WIKIPEDIA SAYS:

Intellectu-alization

A form of rationalization that happens when you remove all emotion from your responses, and flood them with cold, hard, facts like, "I might have forgotten my course today but four riders got disqualified and two others actually fell!"

●● Coping Not Choking

Ego defenses get you into a lot of trouble because they lead you to believe you can hide or avoid disappointing thoughts and feelings, but coping mechanisms can get you out of that trouble by helping you to accept, own, and resolve those thoughts and feelings. The following six coping mechanisms provide healthy and productive ways to confront and solve any challenges.

THAT'S NOT MY JOB!

This is a story about four people named, Everybody, Somebody, Anybody, and Nobody. There was an important job to be done and Everybody was sure that Somebody would do it. Anybody could've done it, but Nobody did it. Somebody got angry about that, because it was Everybody's job. Everybody thought that Anybody could do it, but Nobody realized that Everybody wouldn't do it. It ended up that Everybody blamed Somebody when Nobody did what Anybody could've done. ●

{ 1 } Humor

There are many things you can do when facing adversity, but *humor* (levity) seems to be one of the best options. In fact, Sigmund Freud was once quoted as saying, "Humor can be regarded as the highest of all defensive processes." Levity happens when you cope with challenging emotions by emphasizing amusing or ironic aspects of what happened. Looking for a funny moment or message in a situation that might otherwise make you anxious or nervous can change how your brain interprets the situation. "Thank goodness my face broke my fall," is a great example of using humor as a coping strategy. After all, if you're laughing and smiling, it can't really be that bad!

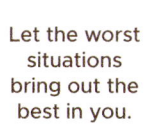

Let the worst situations bring out the best in you.

181

WHAT ARE YOU COMPENSATING FOR?

Compensation is a coping mechanism similar to humility. You're using compensation when you highlight your strengths in the face of weakness like, "I might have forgotten my course, but my equitation was amazing while doing it!" •

{ 2 } Humility

Humble riders don't think too highly of themselves, or too lowly of themselves either. In fact, they seem to have the just right amount of *positive realism* (see p. 81). They make the best of a bad situation without losing their confidence, avoiding it, or looking for scapegoats. Humility allows you to accept disappointment at times when other riders might revert to defense strategies like denial or avoidance. The reason humility acts as such a positive coping mechanism is that it helps you to maintain a realistic self-opinion, thereby, preventing you from developing an over-inflated sense of self-importance that often leads to *ego defenses* (p. 174).

{ 3 } Sublimation

Sublimation happens when you redirect negative emotions into positive, constructive, and empowering behaviors. For example, instead of directing anger toward your horse because you

Fergus BY JEAN ABERNETHY

In any riding scenario, mental stability and physical balance go hand in hand...

Yep. Sometimes they even cancell each other out!

can't seem to stop falling, you channel that energy into a fitness program to improve your leg, seat, and core. The real benefit of sublimation is that you develop the habit of replacing negative emotions with positive behaviors (you redirect bad energy into good things and act *good* when *bad* things happen).

{ 4 } Anticipation

You can anticipate a potentially stressful event in one of two ways: negatively by *worrying* about it or positively by *preparing* for it. Riders who use *anticipation* as a *coping mechanism* always select the latter, mentally rehearsing the efforts they'll make to create favorable outcomes, visual-

THE TRANSFER EFFECT

A phenomenon that occurs is when improving one area of your life automatically triggers a desire to improve other areas. For example, starting an exercise program often triggers a desire to eat healthier food, which, in turn, triggers your mind to feel better about yourself. It's kind of like a BOGO sale for riders! ●

anxiety is a difficult, yet effective method of making that event feel less threatening and bothersome. In fact, the first step in many 12-step programs is to simply accept that you have a problem. Once you've done this, you can move on with the next 11 steps of solving it. Without acceptance, however, it's next to impossible to resolve the challenge (if you can't admit you have a problem, you can't fix it). As long as it's done without judgment or negative commentary (belittling yourself while accepting responsibility will erase the gains) acceptance will do its job of keeping your ego out of the conversation.

izing confidence and courage in the face of adversity, and using self-talk to remind themselves they're capable of overcoming things that might otherwise overcome them. The main idea behind anticipation is that proactively anticipating stressful events (instead of trying to avoid or deny them) makes those events seem more predictable and, therefore, less threatening.

● { 5 } Acceptance

Having the courage to *accept* a situation that has caused (or is causing)

The best way to predict the future is to create it.

- ABRAHAM LINCOLN -
US President

Fergus BY JEAN ABERNETHY

Fergus, can horses think into the past, the present and the future?

Nope.

I couldn't do it last week, I can't do it now...

...and I won't be able to do it tomorrow, either.

{ **6** } Curiosity

Instead of avoiding or denying unwelcome thoughts or events, you might want to consider giving *curiosity* a try. Curiosity happens when you develop a need-to-know attitude about what's happening to you and how you're responding to it. In this way, curiosity is a combination of a coping mechanism and mindfulness. When you become mindful and curious about what's happening, you change your intentions from avoidance to understanding, and understanding is the key to changing any *defense mechanism* into a *coping strategy*.

Six Fixes to Defense Mechanisms

The first step to eliminating *defense mechanisms* is to become mindful that you have other options—choices that include coping strategies like *humor, humility,* and *sublimation*. These alone may be enough to broaden your vision of what coping really means and provide you with a few alternatives when good things start to look bad. If they are not quite enough, however, you can also give the following six tips a try:

Accept what is. Let go of what was. Have faith in what will be.

185

> Falling is
> an accident.
> Staying down
> is a choice.

1. **Don't Get Faked-Out**—Recognize that defense mechanisms just don't work. Avoiding or denying your feelings might give you the false impression they're gone, but they're certainly not forgotten.

2. **Open the Lid**—Defense mechanisms are like a boiling pot with a tight lid. Holding things inside will only increase the pressure your ego will feel. When you feel a defense mechanism starting, remove the lid and let it out.

3. **Be Okay with Not Always Being Okay**—Learn to tolerate uncomfortable thoughts and feelings. Accepting responsibility for your mistakes and mess-ups is possible as long as you're able to be okay with not always being okay.

4. **Soothe Your Stress**—Practice a few self-soothing skills when you start slipping into a defense mechanism. Repeating a mantra like, "Keep calm, ride on," while smiling and taking a few deep breaths might do the trick.

5. **Don't Overspend**—Ask yourself, "What has it cost me to avoid solving my greatest challenges?" Your answers just might convince you that the cost isn't worth the outcome.

6. **Find the Trigger**—When you identify the emotional triggers that cause you to use defense mechanisms (like making a mistake in front of crowds) you take away much of its power. Knowledge is power!

In the end, defense mechanisms create their power through something called *self-deception*. You might think you're doing the right thing (or that you're not doing the wrong thing when you do nothing), but when you take a closer, more honest look, you'll probably agree that defense mechanisms are just an unintentional effort to try and protect your ego. Take this message and allow it to help transform any future defense mechanism into an empowering *coping strategy*. ●

BE
mindful

Your 100% Day

Take a moment to think about a day at the barn. Are you giving and getting 100 percent out of this day? Are you giving it all and getting the results you want? Do you clean your horse's stall but forget to scrub the water buckets? Do you arrive at the show on time but realize you've forgotten your helmet?

Grab a riding friend and try this exercise. Find a seat in the tack room and write the story of your 100-percent day. Give yourself five minutes and write everything you'd accomplish and how it would make you feel, then share it with your friend. Once you've both shared your stories, take a minute to let it all sink in and then step into the barn and make your 100-percent day a reality. ●

GOING THROUGH THINGS
YOU NEVER THOUGHT
YOU'D GO THROUGH
WILL TAKE YOU PLACES
YOU NEVER THOUGHT
YOU'D GO TO.

9

chapter

fears
and tears

9

chapter

Being brave doesn't mean you're never afraid. It means you have the courage to push on and make an effort despite being afraid. It means facing your fears and believing you can overcome them. Bravery isn't the absence of fear; it's the presence of fear without losing faith in your ability to persist. Being brave doesn't mean you're never afraid. It simply means you *believe* in yourself more than you believe in quitting.

Believe it or not, most fears are just an illusion. They're not a physical trait you can see like good posture or a strong leg. They're just something you create in your mind. They're the scary stories you tell yourself and fearful scenes you write and rehearse that make you feel like you're not quite bold, brave, or bright enough to go on. The real problem with fear isn't the fear itself, but the stories and scenes they create. To overcome them, all you have to do is write a different story and rehearse a different scene—but one without the scary ending!

Everyone gets afraid. Riders who say they don't get afraid are just afraid to admit it! After all, riding is a challenging, fast-paced sport done at 20-plus miles an hour on top of 1,200 pounds of strength and strong will. Having a few fears doesn't mean you're weak, not good enough, or a coward; it simply means you've stepped outside your comfort zone where the view can sometimes be a bit intimidating.

As you know from chapter 6, fears are created when your *amygdala* (p. 128) responds to a self-created scary story or scene. Without even thinking about it, your survival instincts kick in and you find yourself fearful and freaking out while fighting and fleeing. While this makes

> Courage means you believe in yourself more than you believe in quitting.

This is not how the story ends. It's simply where it takes a turn you didn't expect.

perfect sense if you're being chased by a polar bear, your amygdala gets it wrong sometimes because not all fears are things you should be afraid of. In fact, there are two very different kinds of fears, and only one of them requires you to fight or flee.

●●● Rational and Irrational Fears

There are two main types of fear: *rational* and *irrational*. *Rational* fears are those that help you identify, assess, and prepare for potentially harmful

Let your courage be stronger than your fear.

dangers and threats (insert polar bear here). *Irrational* fears are those that focus on threats, but not the dangerous or harmful kinds. Becoming mindful of which kind of fear you're facing is the first step to overcoming it.

●● Rational Fears

Rational fear happens when you're afraid something will cause you physical harm or put your life in danger (like a few mares I know!) This is the kind of fear you feel when your horse spooks, bucks, bolts, and jumps out of the arena while you're frantically looking for your reins and stirrups. This is the kind of fear you experience when you slip while standing close to a cliff or are startled by a stranger in a dark alley. This is the kind of fear that protects you by firing your fight or flight survival instincts. Rational fear is good fear.

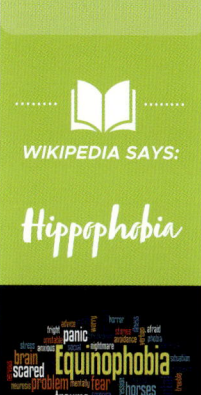

WIKIPEDIA SAYS:

Hippophobia

"Hippophobia" is the fear of horses. It's derived from the Greek words *hippos* (horse) and *phobos* (fear). "Equinophobia" is another term to describe a fear of horses. It combines the Latin word *equus* with the Greek word *phobos*.

Fergus BY JEAN ABERNETHY

Riding provides many opportunities to feel rational fears. Here are a few examples:

- *A dog comes out of nowhere and starts biting your horse's legs between jumps!*

- *Your trailer picks up a scary speed-wobble on the highway when you go a bit too fast!*

- *Your horse unexpectedly stops before a fence and you end up clinging to his neck!*

- *You fall during a trail ride and hear the noise of the other horses coming straight at you!*

- *You run into a bees' nest in the middle of a hack and can hear bees coming for you!*

You might have noticed two interesting things about this list. The first is that rational fear is always unpredictable. That's what makes it so threatening. You never know when your horse is going to stop or when the dogs and bees are going to start. As a result, you never really have the time to physically or mentally prepare for them. The other interesting thing about this list is that every example ended with an exclamation point. That's because the majority of rational fears usually include a scream of some kind!

When a situation provokes a scream, it's likely to also create other fight or flight responses, like holding your breath and tightening your muscles. These are part of the human survival instinct that's been evolving for the last 200,000 years and there's very little you can do about it (even if you wanted to). Your instinct for survival is just too strong. This means that rational fears are *logical* fears that create physical and mental changes so you can protect yourself from threats.

Rational fears are good fears. They keep you safe by protecting you. They are not, however, the kind of fears we spend most of our time talking about. Those fears are called *irrational fears*, and for the most part, they're likely the ones that bother you the most.

●● Irrational Fears

Rational fears protect you from the danger of physical harm (don't stand so close to that cliff!), but *irrational* fears don't include those threats. That why they're called irrational: Your brain fires your survival instinct but you're not facing a threat that puts your survival in danger. Instead, irrational fears are built upon the threat of emotional harm (not physical harm) like the threat to your self-esteem and self-image. As you might have guessed, irrational fears are caused by the *amygdala hijack* (see p. 131).

(see p. 131).

THE SECOND ARROW —FEELING BAD ABOUT FEELING BAD

Most riders know irrational fears are unnecessary, but don't know how to stop them. As a result, it's quite common for riders to feel powerless or foolish (they feel bad about feeling bad). In Buddhism, this is called the "second arrow." The belief is that when you encounter a challenge (like an irrational fear) two arrows will fly your way. The first arrow is the irrational fear, but the second arrow is your reaction to it (feeling powerless or foolish). This second arrow is said to be more painful than the first because it represents suffering, and feeling bad about feeling fearful (even if it's an irrational fear) is what creates that suffering. Learn to accept your fears and work to eliminate them and you can avoid the arrows.●

> "Go boldly
> in the direction
> of your dreams
> and goals.
> Don't allow
> fear to stand
> in your way."
>
> *Henry David
> Thoreau,
> Naturalist,
> Essayist*

There are many different kinds of irrational fears. The *fear of failure* and the *fear of being judged* are two of the most common. Even though they can't harm you physically, your brain prepares for them as if they will. Looking bad in front of others, losing to a competitor, and being judged unfairly can all create a kind of emotional threat that can unintentionally fire your fight or flight response. This is why many riders try to avoid failing or being judged. It's like avoiding standing too close to a cliff. If they can just avoid the threat, they can avoid the danger, but failure and judges aren't dangerous!

Riding provides many opportunities to experience irrational fears. In fact, even though our sport can be physically dangerous, there's a good chance you'll experience more irrational fears than rational ones. Below is a list of 20 common equestrian fears. Can you tell which ones are rational and which ones are irrational? (Hint: the first 16 are irrational!)

COACH STEWART'S NUMBER ONE IRRATIONAL FEAR

CLOWNS.

Notice there's no photo of a clown here. Clown pictures are too scary to put in my book! ●

1. Fear of making a mistake.
2. Fear of not being perfect.
3. Fear of letting down family, friends, trainers, or teammates.
4. Fear of not living up to expectations.
5. Fear of not being as good as your competitors.
6. Fear of not being as good as your horse.
7. Fear of holding your horse back.
8. Fear of hurting your horse.
9. Fear of riding in groups.
10. Fear of going first or last in a class.
11. Fear of being labeled bad.
12. Fear of not progressing as fast as your peers.
13. Fear of being judged.
14. Fear of embarrassment.
15. Fear of losing.
16. Fear of losing a lead.
17. Fear of riding an unfamiliar horse.
18. Fear of riding in the open.
19. Fear of falling.
20. Fear of getting hurt.

If you take a close look at this list you'll notice two interesting things. The first is that irrational fears all tend to be predictable, while rational fears are almost always unpredictable. For example, the fear of failure is simply a *prediction* you might fail, and the fear of being judged is simply a *prediction* the judge might see something you don't want her to see.

The second interesting thing is that all of the 16 irrational fears are caused by *out-grouping* (see p. 20)! Look at the list again—each one of them is caused by worrying about what other people think or comparing yourself to them. As I mentioned in chapter one, changing one thing (out-grouping) can change everything. When you stop worrying and comparing yourself to others, the majority of irrational fears go away.

●●● Causes of Fear

Becoming mindful of what makes you nervous is the first key to overcoming your fears. This is especially true for *rational* fears. Was it a previous fall, or did you see someone injured in a riding accident? Has the ground ever broken a bone or your helmet? This sort of memory can create very threatening images for your brain, so you can't really blame it if it wants to treat it like a fear. Remember, your brain's most important job is survival, and it often tries to keep you safe by making you afraid of something so you'll stay away from it (like that mare you're standing behind!). Let's look at some of the many things that might make you feel a bit fearful.

GO BACK AND FIND WHAT YOU LOST

When you lose your cell phone, you do everything you can to find it. You retrace your steps and search high and low. After all, your phone means a lot to you. You miss it and don't know how you'll live without it. But how much does your confidence mean to you? Does it mean enough to go back and look for it if you lose it? Imagine that you love jumping but a recent fall has you feeling afraid of even cantering. Instead of feeling bad about your setback, go back and find what you lost. Start by finding your courage at the trot, then the canter, then jumping cross-rails and small verticals until you've found what you lost. You'd go back and find your phone because its means so much to you, so why would you feel bad about going back and finding your confidence? ●

⚫⚫ Six Causes of Rational Fears

⚫ { 1 } Bumps, Bangs, and Bruises

Your brain's Number One job is to keep you safe, so imagine how it feels when it lets you fall while jumping a 1,200 pound horse over a four-foot wooden squirrel! Not very good, thank you. This is especially true when you get injured. Once that happens your brain pays special attention and makes lots of notes telling itself to never let you fall again. The way it delivers this message is by making you afraid of jumping.

FEARS AND TEARS!

You've probably seen someone (or been that someone) who burst into tears upon falling from her horse. All your body parts still moved and all your fingers and toes were still there, but something caused you to panic and made it nearly impossible to calm down and get up. That something was adrenaline.

When you experience a situation that threatens your safety, your brain releases adrenaline, and once it hits your system you're going to feel a bit out of control for at least 20 to 30 seconds (even more if you see blood).

Shortness of breath, shaking, and a few tearful sobs all make the situation seem even more intolerable. As a result, many riders often feel embarrassed after such an episode—not because of the fall, but because of their unexpected reaction to it. But remember, this isn't really your fault. It's just the fight or flight reflex causing the unwanted flood of adrenaline. Give yourself 30 seconds to take a few deep breaths so the adrenaline can leave your system, then dust yourself off and get back on. Nothing to see here, folks! ⚫

{ **2** } Seeing is Believing

Your brain will take any excuse to keep you safe. Even watching another rider fall or getting injured is all your brain needs to connect the dots between riding and danger. The more falls and injuries you see, the more likely your brain will say, "See, I told you so!" and the more often you see them, the louder it'll scream!

{ **3** } The Only Thing Predictable Is That He's Unpredictable

Remember that time you rode a horse who wasn't a good match for you? No matter how you asked, he refused to respect your aids or listen to your voice. It was almost like he was dead set on doing the exact opposite of everything you asked. Trying to slow him only made him go faster, and trying to soften his neck only made him lift his head higher. Maybe it was your fault or maybe it was his training (or lack of), but one thing was for sure: your brain didn't like that horse  very much because he was *unpredictable*. Given the choice, your brain would much prefer you to take up tennis, golf, or anything else that does what you ask!

{ **4** } The Need for "Slow"!

Your brain is a pretty good judge of what's harmful, and one of those things is *speed*. In other words, your brain thinks that speed is a threat. It says, if you're going to get in a car accident, make sure you're only going five miles an hour. The slower you go, the safer it feels. This is why it's so difficult to canter again immediately after a bad fall. Your brain says, "Go slow

or get off!" Unfortunately, your brain forgets that you're great at cantering, but makes you fear it in the hopes you'll quit riding and take up tennis, golf, or anything else that goes more slowly!

● { 5 } Getting Older Is a Pain

Remember when you were 10 and thought you were invincible? You could jump off your horse at a gallop or off the roof at the barn, and just knew everything would be okay—because you were 10 and you were invincible! Ah, the good old days. Well that all changed the day you broke your collarbone or got a concussion or bit through your upper lip. From that day on your brain knew you'd have to be more careful because it had proof that you weren't as invincible as you once thought. That was the day you were introduced to the fear of harm.

● { 6 } Getting Smarter Is a Pain, Too!

You were only born with two fears: the fear of loud noises and the fear of falling. This means that all your other fears have been learned over the years, including the *rational* fear of falling

Breathe. Watch. Feel.

The goal of mindful-based thinking is to drop into the present moment. Fear lives in the past and future but cannot survive in the present. So many riders carry around the fall they had yesterday or the anxiety of going off course tomorrow, that it's only natural to ask, "Do they even want to be doing this?" And then you realize that they do. They want it so badly that they're willing to do it afraid. These are some of the bravest riders you could ever meet. So how can you find your "brave"?

- *BREATHE: Your breath is your power, your life force. Your breath acts as an anchor for your thoughts so take deep breaths in and out. Notice the sound your breath makes, the rhythm of your breathing, and the smells around you.*

- *WATCH: Open your eyes and look around. What do you see? Notice your trainer, your friends, your fellow competitors, and your surroundings. Look down at your horse and notice his beauty.*

- *FEEL: In a literal sense, reach down and feel your horse. Feel the texture of his coat and mane. How does your saddle feel? Are both seat bones grounded in the saddle? Take a moment to drop into your body. Feel the experience and check in with your feelings.*

The present moment is always available to you at any time, any day. Next time you find yourself thinking about the rail you had yesterday or getting lost on course tomorrow, remind yourself to just breathe, watch, and feel. ●

and the *irrational* fear of failing. The older you get the more stuff you learn. Some of it is good stuff (like yoga) and some of it's bad (like falling hurts). With age comes knowledge, and with knowledge comes the realization that you get hurt faster and recover slower. Add in a few family obligations like being a mom (I can't get hurt, I have to pick Kevin up at soccer practice in an hour!) and it's easy to see why you might become a bit more fearful with age.

Six Causes of Irrational Fears

{ 1 } Out-Grouping Gets You In Trouble

The overwhelming winner when it comes to creating irrational fears is comparing yourself to others and *wondering, wishing*, and *worrying* what they're thinking about you. As I mentioned in chapter 1, almost all performance anxiety goes away when you stop measuring yourself against others, rid yourself of envy, and learn to value yourself by the effort you gave rather than the outcome you got. When you kick *out-grouping* out of your riding, it'll take most of your irrational fears with it!

{ 2 } Criticism from a Critical Community

All the teachers you've ever had, from your parents to your trainers, have always done their best.

PERFECTIONISM

Trying to be too good for your own good. It hurts knowing you did your best but that your best wasn't good enough, especially if you're a perfectionist. Trying to be perfect in an imperfect world (and imperfect sport with imperfect horses) is like trying to put square pegs into round holes. No matter how hard you try, you'll never succeed. When you learn to measure your self-worth by progress rather than perfection, you'll finally be able to leave the fear of imperfection behind. ●

Their intentions were well-meaning (after all, they only wanted the best for you), but sometimes their message might have gotten a little messed-up in the translation—especially if those messages were interpreted by you as hyper-critical and condemning, mean and demeaning, or belittling or bullying. Not everyone has the patience of an angel or the gift of the gab, so it's easy to see how unintentional messages that promote *out-grouping* ("You're better than her, don't let me down!") and *perfectionism* ("Second place is for first losers!") can cause irrational fears.

{3} Wearing the Wrong Label (and Shoes!)

As you recall from chapter 7, failure is always an event or outcome, but never a person (p. 155). Forgetting this and labeling yourself a failure (just because you failed) is a guaranteed way to create irrational fears. Imagine the pressure (fear) you put on yourself when you think everything has to go right or you'll be labeled wrong. These are some really big shoes to fill. The only problem is, they aren't even your shoes! When you try to squeeze into them, you're bound to feel some pain. Not physical pain, but the emotional kind that makes you believe you're something you're not. Failure is just a thing that happens to you, not a thing that defines you.

{4} Fear of Failure

No one really wants to look bad. For the most part everyone wants to succeed and look good, so it only makes sense that you might feel a little fear of failure from time to time. Even more, you've been told countless times (from people like me!) that mistakes

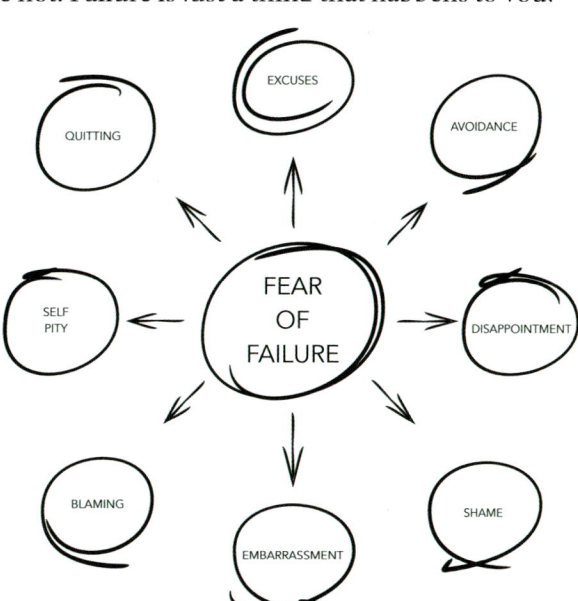

*It's impossible to live
without failing at something.
Unless you live so cautiously
that you might as well not have lived at all,
in which case you fail by default.*

- J. K. ROWLING -
Author

are good learning opportunities, but then you've also been criticized countless times for making mistakes! It's no wonder you fear failure sometimes. The only real problem is that a fear of failure keeps you from leaving your comfort zone (because you're pretty sure failure is on the other side), which limits how much you'll learn and how much success you'll earn.

{5} Fear of Success

No, this isn't a typo. Some riders are actually afraid of succeeding! This gives a whole new meaning to the word "irrational." Riders who fear success aren't actually afraid of success itself, but by the pressure it places on them to keep succeeding or risk being labeled a failure.

— What Kind of Fearful Are You Exercise —

Are you:

☆ The *"First Timer,"* afraid of doing things for the first time, like riding a new horse, cantering, jumping, riding in the open, or showing?

☆ The *"Judge Jittery,"* afraid of being criticized and worried you'll be judged unfairly, given the wrong placement, and that all your hard work will go unrecognized?

☆ The *"Win Worrier,"* afraid of underperforming, losing a lead, being disqualified, forgetting your course, having a poor start, finishing badly, and losing?

☆ The *"People Pleaser,"* afraid of letting people down, not living up to their expectations, looking bad in front of loved ones, and hoping others will do badly so you look good?

☆ The *"Horse Worrier,"* afraid of hurting your horse, holding him back, not being as good as him, not liking him, and worried others won't like him?

☆ The *"Worst Caser,"* afraid of getting hurt, being over-mounted, falling, spooky horses, and getting run away with?

SILLY THINGS THAT RIDERS FEAR

1. Going to a horse show...and forgetting your horse. ●

2. Your horse cutting himself on the shoe he lost in the field last week. ●

3. Forgetting to tighten the girth and sliding off the side of your horse. ●

4. Cutting off your idol in the warm-up arena. ●

5. Falling off your horse...and never seeing him again. ●

6. Putting your new bit on backward. ●

7. Plastic bags. ●

It's like a fear of being built up for a big letdown, or a fear of falling in love because you're afraid you might get hurt. Sometimes, you just need to believe that the risks are worth the rewards.

●●● Fixes for Fears

The problem with fear isn't just the fear itself, but the dread and doubt it creates. It's like looking both ways but still being afraid to cross, or waiting for a life-changing phone call but being afraid to pick it up when it rings. Thankfully, there are many ways to overcome fears and the dread and doubt they cause (so you can finally cross the road and answer the phone!). Here are 10 tips that can help you fix your fears:

●● { 1 } Remember Most of Your Fears Are Irrational

Irrational fears can't harm you (riding in front of a large crowd doesn't threaten your safety or increase the likelihood of getting hurt). They're simply a distraction that robs you of your focus and courage. The next time you're feeling a bit afraid, remind yourself that your fear is most likely harmless and of the *irrational* variety. Remembering this will remove much of the fear's power, which will help you feel safer and more optimistic. When you remove the threat, you remove the fear.

⬤⬤ { 2 } Think SPANKY

When your fears are *rational* (you're afraid your horse is too hyper to jump today), your *amygdala* will likely activate the threat response and make you tight and anxious (just imagine how your horse is going to interpret that!). The next time this happen just remember SPANKY from chapter 6 (p. 135), and smile a little smile, open your shoulders, take a few deep breaths, tell yourself you're excited, be kind to someone, and laugh like a kid. These *silly* coping mechanisms might just help take a little of the seriousness out of the situation so you can regain your confidence.

Doubt is the fertilizer that make fears grow.

⬤⬤ { 3 } Remember the Present Is a Gift

Wondering, wishing, and *worrying* exist in the past and in the future. For example, worrying about your horse not loading into the trailer is just your imagination creating a story that hasn't even happened yet. Fears also live in the future (what if something happens?) and the past (what if something happens again?). You can remove much of a fear's power by changing your mindset from what *has* happened or what *might* happen, to what you can do right now so that it *never* happens!

⬤⬤ { 4 } Find Your Fear Factor

There are two factors that influence the kind of fears you'll experience: *external factors* like the fear of being judged or being beaten by someone else, and *internal factors* like worrying you'll forget your course or

I used to think I had a handle on my emotions...
but then the handle broke off!

FEARS AND TEARS!

You may have heard that eagles teach their young to fly by dropping them and letting them fall. After a few seconds, the mother eagle swoops down, catches the eaglet and lifts it up for another drop. This continues until the eaglet learns to open its wings and control the fall.

But did you know that the lesson actually begins well before the drop? In fact, the first thing the mother eagle does to prepare her young to fly is to remove small sticks and feathers from the nest. Every day the nest becomes smaller and less comfortable. In time, the eaglets find the nest so uncomfortable they decide to leave it, and in doing so, strengthen their muscles and develop their first feelings of independence. Then they get pushed off the cliff! ●

★ MORAL OF THE STORY:

Leaving your comfort zone is the first step to finding your wings and learning to fly.

★ SECOND MORAL OF THE STORY:

Trust your teachers. Your trainers may push you out of the nest by asking you to attempt challenging things, but they'll never ask you to do anything that'll harm you. They'll always be there to catch you.

get eliminated. You might not be able to eliminate all fear factors in your life, but you can certainly remove all the external ones. You have no control over the judge or your competitors so skip thinking of those. You do, however, have control over how you feel about yourself, so work hard to control and eliminate any internal factors.

●● { **5** } Find Your Fear Reactor

Once you've removed the *external* fear factors and identified the *internal* ones that are holding you back, it's time to *react*. This is when you convince yourself you're capable of controlling your fears instead of allowing them to control you. An example of using a *fear reactor* would be when you're afraid of riding in an open space and you *react* by repeating a calming mantra, taking a few deep breaths, and recalling a time when you rode well in an open space. In this example, your fear-reactors were a mantra, deep breathing, and memory motivation.

From the Old English word Grytte, meaning firmness, courage, determination.

●● { **6** } Name It to Tame It

In chapter 7, you learned to avoid labeling yourself a *failure* (p. 155). In the same way, you should never label yourself *afraid*, either. Instead, give your fear a harmless or humorous label that'll make it seem less threatening. One way to do this is to blend words together (like how spoon and fork become "spork" or "foon"). For example, if you have a *fear* of *j*u*dges*, call them "fudges." If you can't come up with a blended word, call the fear of criticism your "critter" or the fear of crowds "stranger-danger." Reframing fears into funny labels changes the way your brain interprets and reacts to them.

May your choices reflect your hopes, not your fears.

- NELSON MANDELA -
Political Leader,
Philanthropist

RECIPROCAL INHIBITION

You can't experience two contradictory emotions at the same time. When you're happy you can't be sad. When you're relaxed you can't be anxious. When you're fearless you can't be fearful. Choose happy, relaxed, and fearless!

●● { 7 } Phone a Friend

The opposite of fear is courage, but you can't call yourself courageous if you're not willing to be vulnerable. Some riders mistakenly think it's

a sign of weakness to admit they're afraid, but it's the opposite! Regardless of whether your fear is rational or irrational, admitting it and seeking help from a friend, family member, or trainer is a sign of courage. This is one of the biggest misconceptions when it comes to fear. A little help can go a long way to removing the weight fear can place on you. Sometimes, it's nice to have someone help you carry it.

●● { 8 } Change It Up

You've heard the saying, "If at first you don't succeed, try, try again," but you also know the definition of *insanity* is doing the same thing over and over again hoping for a different result. So, the next time you're afraid to do something that didn't work in the past, find out what didn't work, and come up with another idea. For example, if you were afraid of cantering last week because you felt unbalanced (and a mantra and deep breathing didn't help), this week come up with a new plan like shortening your stirrups and working on the lunge line for a while.

GOOD AND BAD ARE BOTH GOOD

Most people seek out experiences that are easy and comfortable—in other words, experiences that make them feel good. Unfortunately, this can lead to defining experiences as either good (easy and comfortable) or bad (hard and uncomfortable). Buddhists, however, believe that all experiences, both good and bad, are equal. They're just experiences, and labeling some good and others bad only creates suffering. Fears are usually bundled into the emotions considered bad. But when you remind yourself that fear is just an experience, you can escape much of the suffering it creates. Teach yourself to accept your fear as being neither good nor bad, but instead something that just makes you better. ●

{ **9** } Be Grateful Not Fearful

You can't experience fear and gratitude at the same time. Your brain just isn't designed to create two opposing emotions at the same time. This means that when you learn to be grateful for challenging experiences (even the kind that used to make you a bit anxious), the amount of fear you'll experience will be lessened. It may not go away

gratitude

completely, but the burden it creates will become more manageable. Showing a little self-directed gratitude shifts your focus away from what didn't work in the past (or might not work in the future) to being grateful for what's working in the present.

{ **10** } Be a Good Friend—to Yourself

There's a good chance you find the fears of other people less threatening than the fears you feel yourself. There's also a good chance you believe they're capable of overcoming their fears more easily than you can overcome yours. With this in mind, the next time you get a little afraid, ask yourself what you'd tell a friend. Would it be something like, "I know how strong you are and know you can get through this," or "You've been upset before but it never stopped you"? If so, turn the words around and direct them to yourself. Treat yourself like you would treat a good friend. ●

NOT A TRUE STORY

A magic genie set out to find the world's most courageous person by filling a pool full of sharks and alligators and announcing that the first person to swim across the pool would be granted one wish. After a few seconds, he heard a big splash and saw a man frantically swimming through the sharks and alligators, making it to the other side just in time.

The genie rushed over and said, "You're the bravest man I've ever met! What is your one wish?" The man looked at the genie and said, "I wish I knew who pushed me in!"●

★ MORAL OF THE STORY:

Sometimes fear can make you feel like you've been pushed into situations that you're not completely ready for. When it happens, just keep swimming!

215

3

Bolder, Braver, Brighter

PART THREE

TODAY IS THE
TOMORROW
YOU HOPED FOR
YESTERDAY.

brighter

brighter

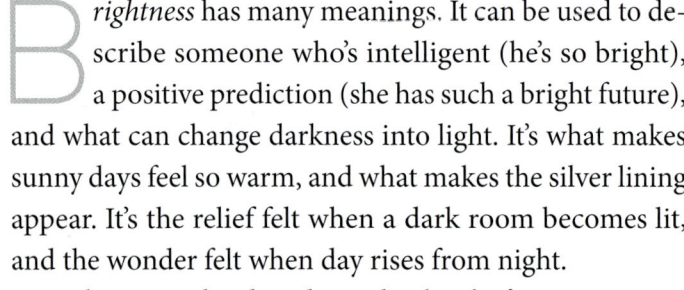

> **Brightness makes the scary go away.**

Brightness has many meanings. It can be used to describe someone who's intelligent (he's so bright), a positive prediction (she has such a bright future), and what can change darkness into light. It's what makes sunny days feel so warm, and what makes the silver lining appear. It's the relief felt when a dark room becomes lit, and the wonder felt when day rises from night.

To become a bright rider with a bright future you must first find the courage to admit you have a few dark tendencies that could use a little lightening. Maybe you compare yourself to others, worry too much about judges, or fear failure, but shining a little light on these tendencies can help bring them out of the dark. Try to repress, avoid, or deny them and they'll continue to hide in that dark place where they'll continue to make you *wonder, wish*, and *worry*. Like the make-believe monster hiding under the bed in a child's room, sometimes a little light is the only thing that can make the *scary* go away.

Bright is the quality
of being filled with
potential to create
a promising future based
on getting through
all the experiences
you've gone through.

••• Mindfulness

Mindfulness brings brightness to the darkness. It's what shines the light of awareness on what you're thinking, how you're feeling, and how you're responding to those thoughts and feelings. It's like turning a light inward so you can finally see how you're acting and reacting, then using that same light to brighten those experiences by accepting them without judging them as right or wrong.

Accepting your thoughts and feelings as natural and normal, observing them without judgment, and redirecting them to more worthy tasks (like the jump in front of you instead of the one on the ground behind you) are the keys to becoming more mindful. They're also the keys to building a brighter future. The more you accept your thoughts and feelings without judgment, the more you can direct them toward more positive and intentional behaviors. Mindfulness is like opening a window and letting in the light so you can finally see what you're made of.

Mindfulness also helps shine a light on your actions and reactions. Regardless of whether they're intentional or not, being mindful allows you to accept mistakes and failures, prevent frustration-filled reprimands of your horse, and

Mindfulness is like looking up at waves from the calmness of the ocean floor. Riding, like those waves, can sometimes feel unpredictable and overwhelming, but mindfulness can help you separate your thoughts and feelings from those waves by allowing you to simply observe them from a deeper place of calmness.

Fergus BY JEAN ABERNETHY

remind you to inhale a cleansing breath instead of exhaling a profanity. Mindfulness is the key to becoming a brighter rider because it's the key to everything that makes you bold and brave.

There are many misconceptions about mindfulness, and one of the most common is that you must always stay in the present moment to do it right. In fact, mindful riders aren't perfect riders either. They lose their focus, experience doubt, and can get distracted or disinterested in the present moment just like everyone else. But mindful riders have control over something

> Before you act, listen. Before you react, think. Before you criticize, wait. Before you quit, try.

Bold and brave riders always see the bright part of any dark situation.

– HANNAH NEFF –
Dressage Rider

Riding can sometimes feel like you're floating down a river with two banks: One bank feels chaotic where things feel out of control and unpredictable, and the other feels rigid where you try to over-control everything. Becoming mindful of these banks can help you float freely down the center of the river without feeling chaos or rigidity.

called the *return*. They can *return* their minds to the present moment once it's strayed, *return* their attention to what they're feeling and experiencing, and *return* their thoughts from random or negative, back to purposeful and positive.

Becoming mindful of any dark thoughts or behaviors is the first step to bringing brightness into your riding. Take a few minutes now and ask yourself if there are any thoughts or behaviors you would like to improve. Perhaps you compare yourself to others, feel like a victim, or have a fixed mindset. Maybe you feel envious of others, magnify your mistakes as if seeing them through a telescope, or feel like a failure just because you failed. Regardless of what they are, the only way to stop them is to start accepting them without judgment as being good or bad. They're just things that happened to you in the past, and things that will help you to become better in the future—as long as you remain mindful of them. ●

MIND OVER MELTDOWN

The ring looks perfect. The jumps are beautifully built with walls and flowers ready to be the backdrop of the ride you've been waiting for. All the hours of hard work finally make sense. Looking over your shoulder, you see the distance to your last warm-up fence. You're in sync with your horse's unwavering rhythm. Your position is solid and as you land, you hear your coach, with approval in her voice, letting you know you're ready for the show ring. You review the course one last time, a pattern that

was once ingrained in your mind, but now all of a sudden it's gone! Where's jump one? Which lead do you start on? Is the last jump the line or the single? Stress-induced amnesia has taken over. Your mind races and your brain-babble reminds you that you've lost control of your course.

It's times like this a little meditation can change meltdowns into mindfulness. Find a quiet place, sit quietly, close your eyes, and bring your attention to your breath. Stay focused on your breathing and accept random thoughts that may come and go. Notice them, let them go, and bring your focus back to your breath. Start slowly with a two-minute meditation and build up to 10 or 20 or more as you become more mindful. Allow meditation to redirect your thoughts back to the positive, clear your mind of the negative, and change mindless thinking into mindful power. ●

— Remove the Sh

Shine a light on the things you'd like to improve by becoming mindful of any thoughts, emotions, or behaviors that might be causing a shadow on your brightness. Remember, negative experiences are just experiences. They're neither good nor bad, they're just experiences.

☆ **Have you ever** experienced *out-grouping* (compared yourself to others, worried about letting someone down, or wished you looked or rode like someone else—p. 20)?

....

☆ **Have you ever** had a *blind-spot bias* (thought people were thinking bad things about you, compared yourself to a finished product, or got stuck thinking of a bad experience—p. 69)?

....

☆ **Have you ever** experienced the *amygdala hijack* (found yourself becoming tense and tight even though you weren't facing a threat that could harm you—p. 131)?

....

☆ **Have memories ever** caused you to doubt yourself (recalled bad memories when you were in a bad mood, or tried to suppress bothersome memories)?

....

adows Exercise—

Read and respond to the questions below. If you can answer and accept them without judgment (feeling bad about them), you'll be taking the first step toward bringing them out from shadows and into the light.

☆ **Have you ever** struggled with being imperfect, making mistakes, or feeling like you're a failure just because you failed?

....

☆ **Have you ever** used a *defense mechanism* (avoidance, denial, or rationalization—p. 173)?

....

☆ **Have you ever** experienced an *irrational fear* (the fear of failure or the fear of being judged—p. 195)?

....

Now that you've had the courage to shine a light on the kinds of thoughts and behaviors you'd like to brighten, take a moment and tell yourself that you *accept* them without judgment and look forward to putting them behind you. Luckily, the next two chapters contain many different tricks, tips, and techniques that can help you do just that.

IF IT WON'T MATTER
IN FIVE YEARS,
DON'T SPEND FIVE
SECONDS WORRYING
ABOUT IT NOW.

10

chapter

brands, breakers, and babble

10

chapter

There's no shortage of things that can take your confidence away, but there's also no shortage of things that can help you get it back. This chapter is written to help you get it back. This chapter is the light that you can shine on the thoughts, emotions, or behaviors you'd love to make a little brighter.

Not only will this chapter introduce you to many tips, tricks, and techniques that can help you overcome things that overwhelm you, it'll also teach you how to remember them at times when you'd normally forget! If you recall from chapter 6, there's a relationship between pressure and memory (p. 149). The more pressure, anxiety, or stress you feel, the more forgetful you become. If the many unique tips, tricks, and techniques in this chapter are going to help you, you're going to have to remember them! Luckily, there are three unique and *forget-proof* programs called *branding, breakers,* and *babble* that can help you do it. Together, they work to help you overcome *wondering, wishing* and *worry*ing so you can become *bolder, braver*, and *brighter*!

●●● Branding

Companies know that to become successful they need to build a strong business brand. It's what promotes their mission, makes their business memorable, and what creates its reputation. Without brand recognition, most companies just wouldn't make it. Equestrians also depend on branding. An *athlete brand* is what helps you stay focused on your mission, stay mindful (memorable) of your goals, and create your own reputation.

●● Your Athlete Brand: Part One

Building an athlete brand is a two-part process. Part One begins with developing three helpful and positive coping tools called *athletic anthems, athletic acronyms,* and *confidence cadences.*

● { 1 } Athletic Anthems

An anthem is another word for music, and music can calm you down, pump you up, and put you in a good mood. But there's a special kind of music that's also been proven to improve your optimism and self-belief. This kind of music is called an *athletic anthem.*

An athletic anthem is a song that improves your optimism and self-belief because its lyrics contain hidden positive-affirmation messages. Messages that remind you to never quit, stay positive, and always believe in yourself. Take the song "The Climb" by Miley Cyrus, for example. When a song delivers an empowering message like this one does, it becomes more than just music. It becomes an anthem.

The first step to building your athlete brand is to take a look in your music playlists to see if any of your favorite songs are athletic anthems. You can do this by performing an online search of the song lyrics to see if there are any positive messages hidden in the words. Most songs don't have the necessary ingredient to be considered an anthem, but you're sure to find a few. Once you do, you can create a riding playlist using those anthems. Perhaps you listen to a few calming,

is life

Ten minutes
of uplifting
music ends
a bad mood
and only
five minutes
improves your
happiness.

yet empowering songs the night before an important ride, and a few upbeat songs the morning of those rides. Here are 10 of my favorite athletic anthems:

- *"Have It All"* by Jason Mraz
- *"Love Myself"* by Hailee Steinfeld
- *"Shake It Off"* by Taylor Swift
- *"Pompeii"* by Bastille
- *"Confident"* by Demi Lovato
- *"Fight Song"* by Rachel Platten
- *"Brave"* by Sara Bareilles
- *"Break My Stride"* by Matthew Wilder
- *"Cowgirls Don't Cry"* by Brooks and Dunn
- *"Try"* by Pink

The power of the athletic anthem comes from the idea that catchy music often gets stuck in your head, and that's exactly what you're hoping for. What could be better than getting positive thoughts and affirmations stuck in your head at times when your thoughts might be less than confident!

{ 2 } Athletic Acronyms

You already know your memory goes down when pressure goes up, but did you know there's a trick that can stop it? That trick is called an *athletic acronym*, and it becomes the second coping tool you'll use to build your *athlete brand*.

Remember that time when you needed to recall several important things on a school test but worried you'd forget them? If you're like many people, you might have tried to come up with an acronym to help you remember them. For example, you can remember the colors of the rainbow by using the acronym ROY G. BIV (red, orange, yellow, green, blue, indigo, violet), or use the acronym PEMDAS to remember the arithmetic order of operations (parentheses, exponent, multiplication, division, addition, and subtraction). In both cases, you might've struggled to remember these lists (especially if you're nervous), but the acronyms help you to recall them.

There are three important rules when building your athletic acronyms: (1) They should remind you who you need to be when you're at your best (confident and/or happy), (2) they should be limited to five or six letters, and (3) they should form complete sentences. The acronym STAR is a good example of a four-lettered athletic acronym. You can use it to remind yourself to *Sit Tall And Relax* (if you're nervous) or *Stop Thinking And Ride* (if you're overanalyzing). As you can see, both acronyms have fewer than six letters, form a complete

HAPPINESS ADVANTAGE

It's a scientific fact that you're better at everything you do when you do it happily because your brain releases feel-good endorphins that make you more confident, courageous, and optimistic. The next time you'd like an extra advantage, try one of these acronyms on for size:

SMILE:
Smiling Makes It Lots Easier

CANDY:
Chill And Never Doubt Yourself

SHAKE:
Stay Happy And Keep Enjoying

SOAR:
Smile On And Relax

LIONS:
Laugh It Off, Never Stop

LOGO:
Laugh Or Get Off

sentence, and remind you who you need to be to be your best. Here are 10 more athletic acronyms you might want to consider when building your brand:

- **BEAR:** *Believe Everything's All Right*
- **Q-TIP:** *Quit Taking It Personally*
- **STRONG:** *Stay Tough, Ride On, Never Give up*
- **FAITH:** *Forget About It, Try Harder*
- **FAST:** *Focus And Sit Tall*
- **ROAR:** *Ride On And Relax*
- **BLAST:** *Breathe, Laugh, And Smile Today*
- **POWER:** *Push On With Every Ride*

{ **3** } Mojo Mantra

In order to ride your best you need to get *in the zone*, and your third coping tool, *cadence training*, is what will help you get there. Before you can get in the zone, however, your brain must first develop something called a *flow state*. This is a sort of relaxed and rhythmical mental sensation that allows your brain to change its thinking from rushed and over-analyzing (called *analysis paralysis*) to effortless and relaxed.

Laughter is like a windshield wiper. It may not stop the rain but it allows you to keep going.

One of the best ways to create this relaxed and rhythmical mental sensation is to repeat a calming and confident *mantra* to yourself (similar to the chants used in yoga, mediation, and mindfulness). I like to call these mantras *mojo mantras* because fears, failures, flaws, and frustrations have a nasty way of robbing you of your mojo!

You've probably used a mojo mantra in the past without even realizing it. Perhaps your trainer asked you to count "1–2, 1–2" when she noticed you becoming a bit tense, or asked you to sing "Row, row, row your boat" when she noticed you worrying or holding your breath. Regardless of the phrase or song, your trainer proved that you can avoid overthinking by simply repeating a relaxing and rhythmical mojo mantra. Here are five examples of mojo mantras you might want to consider using:

- *"Be strong, push on."*
- *"Push on, finish strong."*
- *"Keep calm, ride on."*
- *"Rock, roll, relax."*
- *"You can do it, nothing to it."*

As you can see from this list, many mojo mantras use rhythm and rhyme to create the feeling of flow. Some, however, use humor to break up anxiety and get you into the zone. The only thing better than being in the zone is being in a good mood when you're there! Here are five examples of humorous mojo mantras that I've heard riders use in the past:

- *"Duck, duck, duck, goose"* (repeating *duck* while cantering, and *goose* every time they jump).
- *"Fish are friends not food"* (from Bruce from *Finding Nemo*).
- *"Just keep swimming"* (from Dory in *Finding Nemo*).
- *"Nationwide is on your side…"* (the jingle from the insurance company commercial).
- *"The snack that smiles back"* (the jingle from the Pepperidge Farm Goldfish commercial).

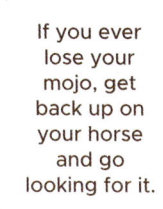

If you ever lose your mojo, get back up on your horse and go looking for it.

GET IN YOUR IZOF

Being in the zone is a shortened version of Individual Zone of Optimal Functioning (or IZOF for short), and it's a good thing because hearing your coach yell, "Get in your individual zone of optimal functioning" takes way too long to say! ●

Using a mojo mantra to *get in the zone* makes you feel like:

- You have complete confidence that your skills match the challenge.

- You feel completely absorbed in the ride and free of distractions.

- You feel immediate feedback and can adjust your tactics effortlessly.

- You have laser-like focus and are free of *wondering, wishing,* and *worrying.*

- You feel as if time slows down so you never feel rushed or pressured.

Perhaps the most important benefit of being in the zone is something called the *autotelic experience,* which is a deep, fulfilling sensation of joy. You no longer wonder, wish, or worry about ribbons, winning or losing, or beating or being beaten. The love of the horse and the joy of the ride become the only rewards you ever need!

●● Your Athlete Brand: Part Two

You've now completed Part One of *building your brand.* You're on your way to creating a play list of empowering athletic anthems, forget-proof athletic acronyms, and calming mojo-mantras. But remember, anxiety and pressure make you forgetful, so Part Two of the *athlete brand* has been created to help you *remember* these three important tools (at times you might otherwise forget them). After all, they can't help you if you forget to use them! Part Two is also made up of three skills: two links and a logo.

● { **1** } Linking Your Tools

The next step in building your *athlete brand* is to link your *anthem, acronym,* and *mojo mantra* together. Your brain has a difficult time focusing on multiple things, so linking them together helps your brain connect them together, making them easier to remember (wired together and fired together). Here's an example of how you can link them together:

- **ACRONYM:** *SUPER (Smile Under Pressure, Enjoy Riding)*

- **ANTHEM:** *"Superman" by R.E.M.*

- **MOJO MANTRA:** *"Up, up, and away"*

As you can see, the acronym, anthem, and mojo mantra are linked together by the idea of Superman. When you think of Superman, your brain naturally thinks of all three. You can now move on to the next step.

● { **2** } Linking Your Body

You know you ride better when your brain and body work together, so your next step in build-

TARGETING

Another way to create the relaxed and rhythmical mental sensation that puts your brain into the flow state (and you into the zone) is by focusing on the rhythmical sounds created by your horse (like the sound of his rhythmical breathing and hoof falls, or the sound of your tack squeaking as he moves). This is called targeting and is what other athletes use to get in the zone (swimmers target their focus on the rhythmical sounds of splashing and cyclists target on the rhythmical sound of their spinning chain). ●

ing your *athlete brand* is to add in a few matching *pre-ride rituals*. Here's an example of how it might look using the Superman example:

- **PRE-RIDE RITUAL 1:**
  *Wearing a Superman T-shirt
  and Superman socks under your riding clothes.*

- **PRE-RIDE RITUAL 2:**
  *Striking a power posture like
  Superman or Wonder Woman.*

You can see how this athlete brand is evolving. The acronym is SUPER, anthem is "Superman," and mantra is "Up, up, and away." You're wearing Superman socks and a Superman T-shirt while standing in a pose like Superman. Everything is linked together by Superman, and your brain loves it!

● { 3 } Logo

Companies work hard to create strong business brands, but they also depend on solid brand (logo) recognition (think Starbucks, Stübben, and Ariat). Your *athlete brand* is no different. Your a*nthem, acronym, mantra*, and *pre-ride rituals* create your brand, but a logo will make it even more memorable. On the left is an example of a logo that would match the Superman brand.

●● Shifting to Chunking

Your brain learns new skills by shifting your attention from one task to another, but over time, your brain realizes that many skills are related, so it chunks them together into one new skill (instead of several old ones). Bridling your horse is a good example. In the beginning, you struggled putting on the bridle because you had to think of the many required steps, but over time your brain noticed you always did the same steps in the same order, so it *chunked* all those steps together into one new skill. You no longer need to remember the many steps, you simply *bridle* your horse without thinking about it.

One of your first experiences with the shifting-to-chunking model occurred when you learned to tie your shoelaces. This holds true for building your brand. In the beginning, you may need to focus on your *anthem, acronym, cadence,* and *pre-ride rituals,* but with a little time and practice they should become chunked together. This means that when you see the Superman logo on the saddle pad, you'll automatically think of all your tools (without even trying to remember them) because your brain will have *chunked* them together. Once again, *when behaviors are wired together, they're fired together.*

●●● Bringing It All Together

You now know how to build an *athlete brand,* but how does it actually work? Well, imagine one day feeling so anxious that you forget your anthem, acronym, mantra, and pre-ride rituals (that's what pressure does, after all), but then you see the Superman logo on your saddle pad. Upon seeing it, it jogs your memory and you to say, "Smile Under Pressure, Enjoy Riding" (*acronym*) and "Up, up and away" (*mantra*) while striking a Superman power posture and taking a peek at your Superman T-shirt under your show jacket (*pre-ride rituals*).

In this example, the Superman logo on the saddle pad acted as a visual reminder for your anthem, acronym, mantra, and pre-ride ritual. This kind of reminder is called a *mental trigger* because it triggers your brain into remembering important things at a time when you might otherwise forget. For this reason, it would be great if you could put your logo in as many places as possible (on your saddle pad, tack trunk, and trailer door). The more you see it, the more your brain will be triggered to remember your brand.

237

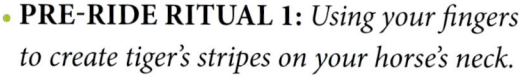

Here are three ways a logo can help trigger your brand, in this case, Roar.

⚫⚫ Time to Build Your Brand

Let's get started building your brand. Take your time and don't be surprised if it takes a little longer than expected. The good news is that even if it takes you five hours or five days, that time will be spent thinking positive thoughts as you look for acronyms, anthems, cadences, and pre-ride rituals that remind you to finish strong, never give up, and enjoy the ride!

Building your brand can be tricky because it's a bit of a puzzle with lots of pieces, so here is another example that might help you figure out how to fit all your pieces together:

- **BRAND:** *Roar*

- **ANTHEM:** *"Roar" by Katy Perry*

- **ACRONYM:** *ROAR (Ride On And Relax)*

- **MANTRA:** *"Hear me roar…Hear me roar…"*

- **PRE-RIDE RITUAL 1:** *Using your fingers to create tiger's stripes on your horse's neck.*

- **PRE-RIDE RITUAL 2:** *Taking a tiger teddy bear to the show grounds.*

- **LOGO:** *A tiger head inside a circle over the top of the word ROAR.*

– Build Your Athlete Brand Exercise –

Now that you've seen several athlete brands in action, try building your own.

☆ **Chose** an athletic **anthem** (a song with a hidden positive message in the lyrics):

....

☆ **Chose** a matching **athletic acronym** (five letters or fewer forming a sentence):

....

☆ **Chose** a matching **mojo mantra** (it has to have rhythm and rhyme):

....

☆ **Chose** two **matching pre-ride** rituals:

1. ....

2. ....

☆ **Draw** a rough drawing of your brand's logo:

YOU'RE NOT DONE UNTIL YOU'RE DONE...

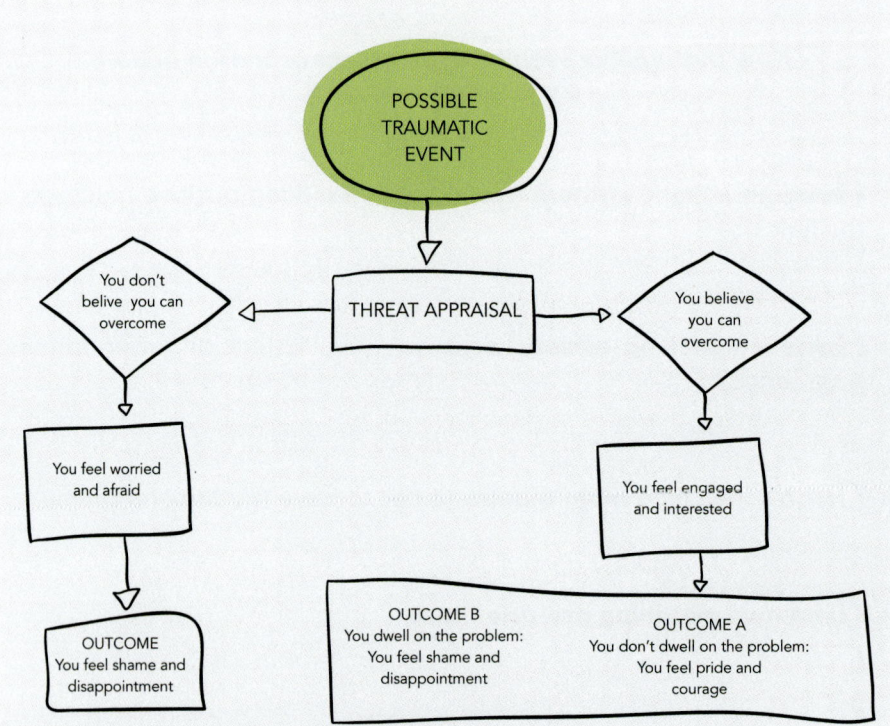

Breaking bad habits happens in three phases. You must first begin with the strong belief that you're capable of overcoming challenges and capable of achieving great things (that you're equal to the task). You must then continue to believe in your abilities while performing the skill (even when things don't go as planned). You must then also be able to shake off any guilt or disappointment after the effort, because if you dwell or ruminate about the problem afterward, it'll undo all the gains previously achieved (even if you were able to remain positive before and during the effort). ●

●●● Breakers

Breaker is short for *pattern-breaker*, which is the intention to *break* old bad habits (or thought patterns) and replace them with more positive new ones (and making those new habits forget-proof, even when nervous). Replacing the habit of saying, "I'm nervous" with "I'm excited" is a good example of how a little pattern-breaker can make a big difference. There are four steps to building your breaker: *time, tasks, triggers,* and *tags*.

●● Time

You don't just get nervous before an important class, clinic, or competition. Sometimes, you get nervous way before a ride, in the middle of it, and sometimes even after it's over! As a result, you should consider building three breakers, one for each of the following time periods:

- **PRE-RIDE BREAKER:**
  Develop new habits before your class, clinic, competition.

- **PRIME-RIDE BREAKER:**
  Develop new habits in the middle of your class, clinic, competition.

- **POST-RIDE BREAKER:**
  Develop new habits after your class, clinic, competition is over.

●● Tasks

Tasks are similar to the coping tools you built for your *athlete brand*, but you have many more options when it comes to *breakers*. *Tasks* are basically any positive behavior (habit) that

TRUE STORY

Did you know that army ants have been known to walk in circles until they die? This ultimate self-defeating behavior results from worker ants following the pheromone trails of other ants while leaving their own trail for others to follow. Unfortunately, if these trails cross and form a loop, the ants become trapped in an endless circle, following each other until they succumb to exhaustion or dehydration! All they have to do to break the cycle (and the circle!) is to simply break the pattern (habit) that's harming them. ●

★ MORAL OF THE STORY:

Like ants, you might also have a few self-defeating patterns (habits) that deserve to be broken (such as feeling like a failure just because you failed). The ants find themselves trapped in a vicious cycle they can't break because it loops back onto itself. Emotions like worry and doubt work in much the same way, often looping back onto themselves so you can't seem to break the pattern of worrying and doubting yourself. All the ants need to do is break the pattern to find their freedom. All you need to do is break the pattern to find your fearlessness.

you do at a *time* when you're feeling nervous. Obviously, the role of your *task* is to make anxious *times* feel better. Here are eight examples of tasks you might want to consider using:

- Take several deep, relaxing breaths (see *adrenaline breath*, p. 138).
- Open your shoulders while sitting tall and confident (see *power posture*, p. 137).
- Smile (see SPANKY, p. 135).

- Repeat a *mojo mantra* (see p. 232).
- Think of a positive memory from your past (see *memory motivation*, p. 149).
- Listen to calming and/or empowering music (see *athletic anthems*, p. 229).
- Show gratitude by thanking someone (see the *gratitude mindset*, p. 94).
- Repeat an empowering acronym (see *athletic acronyms*, p 230).

*When was the last time
you did something for the first time?*

●● Triggers

This is the stage that gives your breaker its power. A *trigger* is anything that *triggers* your brain into doing your *tasks* at a *time* you're feeling nervous. When done correctly, whenever you experience the *trigger*, you'll automatically do the *task* without even thinking about it. It will just happen automatically. The

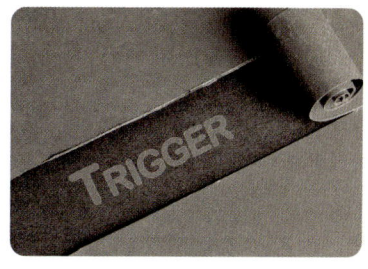

task and the *trigger* will be wired together and then fired together. This is the stage that makes breakers *forget-proof.*

Here's a story to help you to understand triggers: Famous physiologist and doctor Ivan Pavlov discovered that dogs would salivate when given tasty food, but that they could also be taught to salivate at the sound of a bell when that bell was rung at the same time they were given the food. After a while, he discovered that

243

the dogs would salivate at the sound of the bell, even when the food wasn't given. He concluded that the dogs were using the sound of the bell as a *trigger* to think about the food. They didn't need to see the food to salivate any more, they just needed to hear the bell to be reminded of it. The bell and food now wired and fired together.

You can certainly use the sound of a bell as a trigger to drool, but you might want to consider using your *breaker* to remind you to do something a bit more useful. Here's a good example:

A nervous dressage rider told herself to take a deep breath, open her shoulders, and smile every time she heard the ding of the 45-second bell before a dressage test (what she called being a BOSS—an acronym for Breath, Open Shoulders, and Smile). Upon arriving at the showgrounds she heard someone else's bell and did her BOSS. Ten minutes later she heard another bell, five minutes after that she heard another, and ten minutes after that, she heard her own bell, and all three times she took a breath, opened her shoulders, and smiled.

What was surprising was what happened the next day. She found herself doing the same thing every time she

heard the microwave *ding* and the elevator button *ring*! It didn't take long before her brain started using the *ding* as a trigger to take a deep breath, open her shoulders, and smile—regardless of where the ding came from! The sound of the bell and her new habit were now wired and fired together (the same way the sound of the bell worked for the dogs). She no longer needed to remember it; it was now an automatic habit and *forget-proof*!

Here's the neat part: In the past, she was nervous, tense, and tight at horse shows, but her *breaker* helped her become more positive, confident, and successful. This was all because her brain was using a sound to *trigger* her brain into doing her *tasks* at a *time* she felt nervous. It was like drooling at the sight of food—only better!

● Five Kinds of Triggers

Triggers can be divided into one of five categories: *sounds, movements, individuals, locations,* and *emotions.* This means that you can trigger your brain into doing your tasks automatically every time you hear something, do something, see someone, go somewhere, or feel something. Below are several examples. Feel free to use some of these, or come up with a few of your own.

1. **Sound Triggers**—The ding of the dressage bell, snapping of your helmet strap, your class being called over the loud speaker, the slapping of the leathers as you pull your irons down, the wind as you pick up your canter—and what I like to call "mom gasps"!

2. **Movement Triggers**—Mounting, pulling on your boots and helmet, shortening your reins, riding a courtesy or 10-meter circle, jumping a fence, halting at X.

3. **Individual Triggers**—Judges, friends, family members, opponents, volunteers, spectators, and your trainer. You can even use your horse as a trigger (horses are people, too). If you're accident-prone, maybe the paramedic should be your trigger!

4. **Location Triggers**—Passing a letter in dressage (C or M), the first fence on the jump course, the mounting

block, cross-country start box, in-gate, inside the stall, corners, and the dreaded warm-up arena.

5. **Emotional Triggers**—Feeling envious, comparing yourself to others, embarrassment, anger, fears (of failure, for example), frustration

245

The halt in dressage is a perfect movement (and location) trigger for all your positive tasks.

(FRANKY), and when you say, "Dang it!" (or whatever other four-letter word you say after making a mistake!).

FRUSTRATION

As you can see, there's no shortage of things you can use as *triggers,* but if you look at the list below, you might notice something interesting—they all come together to form the acronym

HAPPY *smile* :)

SMILE. Regardless of the *task(s)* you decide to use, consider making one of them a little smile. After all, you should take your happiness every bit as seriously as the other parts of your riding. Remember, be happy in your happy place!

Sound
Movement
Individual
Location
Emotion

The quokka is considered the happiest animal on the planet because of its ever-present smile. The next time you're having a hard time finding your smile, just think of this little guy and channel your inner quokka.

Tags

Using a *trigger* so your brain focuses on the positive in negative situations (does good *things* at bad *times*) is the goal of your *breaker*, and the more you practice it, the more automatic and effortless it'll become. That's where your *tag* comes in. The word *tag* is commonly used as a synonym for graffiti. It's an image, a picture, or visual representation of something important (just like the logo used to build your *athlete brand*). Creating your tag is a four-step program:

1. **Decide** what your tasks are going to be—for example, *Breathe, Laugh, And Stay Tough.*

2. **Create** an acronym to match your tasks. In this case it would be BLAST.

3. **Find** an image (your *tag*) that represents BLAST. A cartoon image of a stick of dynamite would work nicely here.

4. Like your *logo*, stick your dynamite image on your tack trunk, saddle pad, tack-room wall, and trailer door. The more you see your *tag* (the dynamite), the more likely you'll remember to *breathe, laugh, and stay tough.*

●● Three Examples of Breakers

Having a hard time finding your *times, tasks, triggers,* and *tags*? Not quite able to build your breaker yet? No worries. Below are three examples that might help you to build your own:

Have a blast today.

TIME: *Pre-Ride Breaker*
TRIGGER: *Entering the warm-up arena (location trigger)*
TASK: *Breathe and say YOLO (You Only Live Once)*
TAG: *An image of an "EASY" button (Exhale And Say Yolo!)*

TIME: *Prime-Ride Breaker*
TRIGGER: *Horse pulling a rail (movement trigger)*
TASK: *Take a deep breath, smile, and say, "Buzz, buzz"*
TAG: *An image of a BEE (Breathe, Exhale, Enjoy)*

TIME: *Post-Ride Breaker*
TRIGGER: *Nervously approaching your trainer after a disappointing ride (individual trigger)*
TASK: *Telling your trainer you did your best*
TAG: *An image of a BEAR (Best Effort And Relax)*

I hope these sample breakers will help you build your own. Remember, you're not limited to a single time, trigger, task, or tag. For example, a breaker can use several of each. Let's say you are worried about being judged (what the judge will see, think, and score). You can: thank the judge before you

– Build Your Breaker Exercise –

You'll only need three things to build your breaker:
(1) A little patience, (2) a lot of creativity, and (3) even more courage,
because you'll need to have the confidence to admit that you're not
perfect (that there are things that take your confidence away).
Remember, you can't call yourself courageous unless
you're willing to be vulnerable.

☆ **Time:**   **PRE-RIDE BREAKER**

☆ **Trigger:** ....

☆ **Tasks:**   1................. 2................. 3.................

☆ **Tag:**   Acronym: .... Image: ....

☆ **Time:**   **PRIME-RIDE BREAKER**

☆ **Trigger:** ....

☆ **Tasks:**   1................. 2................. 3.................

☆ **Tag:**   Acronym: .... Image: ....

☆ **Time:**   **POST-RIDE BREAKER**

☆ **Trigger:** ....

☆ **Tasks:**   1................. 2................. 3.................

☆ **Tag:**   Acronym: .... Image: ....

ride (gratitude as a task); take a deep breath when you hear the 45-second bell (sound trigger); smile at the judge when you halt at X (movement trigger); repeat a mojo mantra when you proceed toward C (location trigger); and then open your shoulder every time you think of the judge (individual trigger).

●●● Babble

The words you say to yourself have a big impact on your attitude and ability. The *doors of opportunity* open when they're positive, but remain tightly closed when they're negative. *Brain babble* (also referred to as self-talk, internal dialogue, or thought chatter) is what helps you to keep those doors from slamming on you.

Brands and *breakers* train your brain to automatically focus on positive thoughts and actions (wiring and firing together) and to remember them during times of stress. *Brain babble* does the same thing, and it's a good thing because you think up to 60,000 thoughts every day (one about every 1.5 seconds) so imagine if even a small portion of them are doubtful or fearful. Unfortunately, your brain is very good at thinking really bad things, but you

My veterinarian says I have a delicate nervous system...

...but she doesn't take into consideration that the grass is always greener on the other side of the electric fence!

WIKIPEDIA SAYS:

Mental Filtering

A mechanism in your brain that gives greater importance to negative thoughts than positive thoughts. It's part of your survival instinct (focus on threats and you might survive!) but you can change it by using one of these tricks:

PRIMACY EFFECT:
Your brain remembers the first thing it hears best, so always tell yourself what you did well before telling yourself what you did poorly.

RECENCY EFFECT:
Always finish on a good note because your brain gives priority to your most recent experiences. This is why you never end your horse's training session on a bad note.

SANDWICHING:
When recovering after a mistake, give yourself a quick compliment, followed by the criticism, and then another compliment. Sandwiching the criticism between two compliments allows your brain to accept the criticism without being threatened by it.

can change this by becoming more mindful of any *bad* babble, stopping it, and replacing it with more positive thought options. This three-part technique is called *thought-stopping* and it's a great way to keep the *door of opportunity* propped open.

●● Step 1: Thought Recognition

The first step to stopping negative brain babble is to recognize you're doing it (you can't fix what doesn't feel broken). This is another example of how important it is to be mindful of your thoughts. *Bad* babble typically comes in two forms: tricky (like saying you'll *try* to do your best instead of saying you *will* do your best), and toxic (like telling yourself you're a failure just because you failed). If you can tune into your self-talk and identify any tricky or toxic talk, you can move on to the next step of stopping it.

●● Step 2: Thought Removal

Once you discover it, you can disrupt and remove it. That's the role of a *thought-remover* (or *thought-stopper*), and it works by simply say-

ing a pre-determined *code word* (to yourself) to stop the flow of unwanted babble. In other words, every time you recognize you're thinking a bad thought, you say (or yell!) to yourself a code word so that it startles your brain into stopping and removing the tricky or toxic talk. The words "Whoa!" or "Halt!" are common thought-removers and stoppers for equestrians because they're often used to stop things (like your horse!), but humorous words like "critter" (recognizing you're being self-*critical*) or acronyms like STAR (Stop Thinking And Relax) are just as good.

● Verbal Eraser

Little things can have a big impact on your brain babble, and the word *but* is one of those little things! The word *but* is part of a unique family of words called *verbal erasers*, which are basically bad words that erase good things. Here are a few examples:

- *I know I'm a good rider, but everyone is so much better.*
- *My first few fences were great, but the last one was horrible.*
- *I know failure is a part of riding, but I feel like such a failure.*

As you can see, the word *but* erases the first portion of the statement (the good part). This happens because words spoken after a verbal eraser are interpreted by your brain as more important than those that occurred before it. The next time you have something good to say about yourself, put the eraser away and just end after you've said it.

Little things can make a big difference. If you don't believe it, try sleeping in a room with a mosquito.

253

●● Step 3: Thought Replacement

Now that you've stopped the *bad* babble, your mind will be looking for a replacement. Remember, your brain can't go for more than a second or two without thinking, so this is your chance to swap the bad for good. The thought you decide to use as a replacement should be memorized, rehearsed often, and give you a clearly defined plan of action. The acronym BOSS (from your *breaker*) is a good example. Once you've stopped and removed the bad babble, you say to yourself *Breathe, Open Shoulders, and Smile*, or ROAR (from your brand) to *Ride On And Relax*. Who said you can't mix your brands, breakers, and babble?

● Recognize, Remove, Replace, and Repeat!

Make your *thought replacement* even stronger by repeating it several times, and each time, place the emphasis on a different word (placing the emphasis on the first word the first time, the second word the second time, and so on). For example, if your thought replacement is BEAR (*Believe Everything's All Right*), repeat it four times, and each time shift the emphasis to the next word. It'll look like this:

BELIEVE IN *yourself*

BELIEVE *everything's all right.*
Believe **EVERYTHING'S** *all right.*
Believe everything's **ALL** *right.*
Believe everything's all **RIGHT**.

Before finishing up, repeat the entire sentence again, only this time place the emphasis on all four words (as if confidently yelling it to yourself). In the end, you'll have repeated your *thought replacement* five times, which is

MAKE YOUR OWN WORD CLOUD

This is a word cloud, and it is easy to make. Start by writing the central message of your cloud in bold letters (like courage, believe, or fearless), then write as many synonyms as you can. Once you've run out of ideas, open an online thesaurus and find more. Once your list is complete, type the ideas in a variety of fonts and colors, and print and tape it to your wall, tack trunk, trailer door, or any other place you pass often. ●

what'll begin to make this new *better brain babble* so *forget-proof*!

Here's a good example of a *thought-stopper* that can help you *recognize, remove,* and *replace* any bad thoughts with more positive replacements.

1. You *recognize* you're feeling envious of another rider.

2. You *remove* the negative thought by yelling the word "FLY" to yourself.

3. You *replace* the old negative thought with the acronym "FLY" (*First Love Yourself*).

4. You *repeat* the phrase *First Love Yourself* three times, each time placing the emphasis on the next word.

5. You finish up by repeating *First Love Yourself* once more, only this time emphasizing every word.

Now it's your turn to build your own babble! The next time you *recognize* you're thinking *bad* babble, *remove* and *replace* it with the following:

Thought Remover: ....

....

....

Thought Replacement: ....

....

....

255

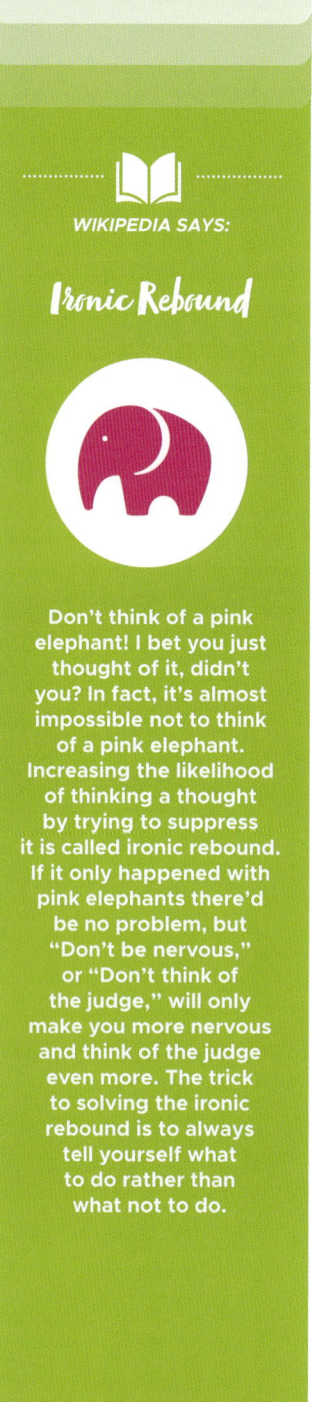

So, How I Will Get to Thank You… Yet

This "sentence" makes no sense, and I'm sure my publishers think I'm going crazy, but this isn't actually a sentence (and I'm not going crazy!). It's a six-part, brain-babble program that can help you become *bolder, braver*, and *brighter*. Let's discuss each of the six components, one at a time.

1. **So**—*What-if* thinking is bad. For example, "What-if I fail or fall?" The next time you think a *what-if* sentence, put the word *so* in front of it. "What if I fail or fall" turns into "*So* what if I fail or fall?" Finish your new sentence by adding a positive *follow-up* sentence at the end, like "So what if I fail or fall, *I'll get up and keep trying until I get it right.*"

2. **How**—Brain babble works best when you ask yourself *how* to achieve something rather than telling yourself what to achieve. For example, "How can I relax?" is much better than saying, "Stop freaking out!" because your brain responds to *how* questions by seeking answers to them (like taking a deep breath).

3. **I Will**—Brain babble also works better when you tell yourself what you *will* do, instead of what you *won't* do. For example, "I *will* take a deep breath and relax," is better than saying, "I *won't* be nervous." Your brain works by creating mental pictures of what you're thinking, so help it to form positive images by giving it some positive thoughts.

4. **Get To**—The words *have to* change opportunities into obligations. "I *have* to go to the barn," and "I have to work on my leg," make you feel like you have no choice. Replace them with *get to* or *love to* and the babble becomes, "I *get to* go to the barn, and I *love to* work on my leg," (you change the obligation back to an opportunity). You can even replace them with *like to*, *proud to*, and *happy to* if you want!

5. **Thank You**—You thank other people over 5,000 times a year but never thank yourself (especially after mistakes and failures). You can remove disappointment from your riding by simply thanking yourself after every effort and error you make. These two simple words can trick your brain into feeling good about those efforts and errors, even if the outcome wasn't what you'd hoped for.

6. **Yet**—There are many things you can't do, but telling yourself *you can't do them* is only half the story. Complete your story by adding the word *yet* to the end of the sentence: "I can't sit his trot," or "I can't do flying changes," becomes, "I can't sit his trot *yet*," or "I can't do flying changes *yet*." This helps your brain get excited about what's in your future! ●

> By the time you turn 17 years old, you've heard the word "No" 150,000 times, but you've only heard the word "Yes" 5,000 times. Maybe that's why it's so much easier to tell yourself what you can't do rather that what you can do. Brain babble is a numbers game!

11

chapter

buckets, barriers, and bamboo

11

chapter

When you arrive at the barn you arrive at a place that's more than just fences and fields. You arrive at your happy place. The place you go when you need a little distraction from the craziness of a crazy world. Unlike other sports, however, your happy place isn't defined by the playing field, but by the relationships with your trainers, peers, and horses found there.

But what happens when your happy place becomes a little less than happy? What happens when your thoughts turn from friends, fillies, and fun, to fears, failing, flaws, and freaking out? What happens when they turn from calm, cool, and collected, to mistakes, missed opportunities, and messing up? What happens when they turn from joy to jealousy or from resiliency to regret? What happens when your happy place turns into your crappy place? That's where the stories of *buckets, bamboo,* and *barriers* come in.

● ● ● **Buckets**

 A trainer filled a bucket with sponges and asked her students if it was full. They all said yes, so she took a box of bit-keepers and poured them into the bucket, filling in the spaces between the sponges. She asked again if the bucket was full. Feeling a little silly they'd been tricked, they all agreed it was, until the trainer poured sand into the bucket, filling in all the spaces between the bit-keepers. She asked again if the bucket was full. Cautious about being tricked a third time, they replied somewhat tentatively, "Yes, it's full now." The trainer then poured water into the bucket, filling all the space that remained. "Now," she said, "the bucket is full."

The bucket in this story is a metaphor for your riding life. The sponges and bit-keepers represent *positive* emotions like confidence, pride, optimism, commitment, self-respect, self-belief, and self-esteem. These are the things that make you *bolder, braver,* and *brighter.* The sand and water represent *negative* emotions like fear, envy, shame, doubt, regret, denial, avoidance, limiting-beliefs, and blind-spot bias. These are the things that make you *wonder, wish,* and *worry.*

If you ride in a way that puts the negative sand and water in your bucket *first,* there won't be any room for the positive bit-keepers and sponges. Feeling like a failure because you failed, comparing yourself to others, or dwelling on mistakes will simply take up all the room that deserves to be left for the things that really matter, like your confidence, courage, and self-respect.

In the future, always remember to fill your bucket first with the sponges and bit-keepers of *bolder, braver,* and *brighter,* instead of the sand and water of *wondering, wishing,* and *worrying.*

> The best
> medicine for
> a horse is love.
> If it doesn't
> work, increase
> the dose.

●●● Barriers

Belief barriers are thoughts and behaviors that hold you back from achieving what you deserve. *Limiting beliefs, out-grouping, defense mechanisms,* and *fears* are belief barriers. They're called "barriers" because they place walls between you and what you can accomplish—walls that make you believe you're not bold enough, brave enough, or bright enough to succeed. They are more prevalent in riding than in other sports because of the unpredictable nature of horses. The walls around riders come in an endless variety of shapes and sizes. I've spoken about many belief barriers in this book, including:

- Fears, failure, flaws, frustration, and freaking out.
- Mistakes, missed opportunities, messing up, and memories.
- Disappointment, doubt, dejection, and defense mechanisms.
- Run-outs, refusals, and regrets.
- Struggles, setbacks, and shame.
- Biases, broken mirrors, and body envy.
- (Not to mention judges' glares, spectators' stares, and chestnut mares!)

263

*Live a life you don't need
to take a vacation from.
Besides, you're into horses
so you can't afford to go on
vacation anyway.*

THE WALL

Three riders go for a walk and notice their trainer standing in front of a large wall. As they approach, the trainer says there are many amazing rewards on the other side of the wall but that it'll take hours of hard work to get over. She also says she believes all three are capable of it but that they'll need to believe in themselves as much as she believes in them.

The first rider approaches the wall and ponders the challenge it presents. She then looks back to her trainer and says, "Nope, I can't do it," and turns and walks away. The second rider doesn't even look at the wall; she just looks at her trainer and says, "Well if she can't do it, I can't do it," and walks away. But then the third rider approaches the wall, thinks about it, and unexpectedly takes off her hat and throws it over the wall. She then looks back at her trainer and says, "Well, now you and I need to work together to get me over that wall—I have to go and get my hat back!"

Sometimes in life you might need a little extra motivation to get over the walls standing between you and your rewards. The next time you encounter a belief barrier, let the love of the horse (and the love of our sport) be the hat that gets you over your wall. Our sport is full of barriers and walls that will try to hold you back, but none of them will ever be as big as your love of the horse. ●

The first step in avoiding or overcoming *belief barriers* is to always remember these three important words:

1. **Laugh**—Take your happiness as seriously as you take the rest of your sport.

2. **Learn**—Ask yourself what previous barriers (failures and mistakes) have taught you.

3. **Love**—Remind yourself that you didn't start riding to win ribbons. You started for the love of the horse.

No wall is as big as your love for your horse.

The second step in avoiding or overcoming belief-barriers is to read this brief story called "The Wall" (see sidebar).

*Remember
how far you've come,
not just how far
you have to go.
You may not be
where you want to be,
but neither are you
where you used to be.*

●●● Bamboo

There's a special tree called the Chinese bamboo. What makes this tree so unique is that you plant it and water it for four years…and absolutely nothing happens! It won't grow or even sprout a leaf to give you the indication that it's considering growing. If you're like most people, you'll become impatient, believe something's wrong, and think it'll never grow. And then you'll probably give up and start looking for a better tree to plant.

But something extraordinary happens in the fifth year: The Chinese bamboo grows to a height of 90 feet in one year! It grows so fast that you can actually see and hear it grow if you have the patience to pay attention!

You see, what you didn't realize is that for the first four years the Chinese bamboo was growing entirely underground. Hidden deep below the surface for all those years it had been growing a massive root system because it knew it could never grow to its full potential without first building a strong foundation. Sometimes riding can feel a bit like the Chinese bamboo. Many riders wish they could just skip the first four years and get on with the fifth. Maybe you feel like you've been putting in the time but don't really think anything is changing. Maybe you wish you could skip the basics and jump ahead to the big stuff. Maybe you feel like all your hard work and effort isn't paying off because you're still making mistakes. Maybe you'll become impatient, believe the efforts aren't worth it, and think it's never going to happen.

But before you believe any of this, remind yourself what's really happening here. The time you're dedicating to learning the basics is what's building the foundation that your future growth and success depends on. Like underground roots, your efforts to overcome fears and failures, envy and shame, and doubt and defense mechanisms are what will ultimately create the framework that'll carry you toward achieving true success and self-satisfaction. Without the years of growth under the surface, you'll simply never be able to reach your true heights.

Your efforts and errors are the key to building your foundation, and the keys to becoming *bolder, braver,* and *brighter.* ●

4

THE TWO MOST
IMPORTANT DAYS
IN YOUR LIFE ARE
THE DAY YOU WERE
BORN AND THE DAY
YOU FIND OUT WHY.

best

best

●●● The Six Most Important Words You'll Ever Say

The next time you experience *wondering, wishing,* and *worrying,* and the next time you're feeling *less* than *bold, brave,* and *bright,* repeat these six words to yourself:

I'm going to do my best.

While you've said them before, they're perhaps the most important words you can ever say to yourself. Anxiety is usually a sign you're worried about performing poorly or letting someone down, but *anyone who loves you* only wants one thing from you. They only want you to do your best. They don't need you to always *be* the best or better than the rest. They simply want you to *do your best.*

When you understand and accept this, the pressure you've been feeling will subside. No longer will you have to chase the tail of the unrealistic expectation of having to be perfect to be valuable. You'll no longer feel the burden of having to live up to someone's expectations or worry about letting someone else down. You'll realize that you're no longer being measured by your outcomes but by your efforts.

You can also use these words to lessen the sting of a disappointing ride. Telling your trainer or loved one that you *did your best* (even if you failed) is all they (and you) ever really need to know, because all they (and you) could ever ask of you is that you *did your best*.

This book has discussed many things that can cause anxiety, and many things that can combat them, but of the 49,500 words in the book, perhaps the most important of all are simply:

I'm going do my best.
I did my best.
I am bolder. I am braver. I am brighter.

● ● ●

LIVE LIFE AS IF SOMEONE LEFT THE GATE OPEN.

– a c k n o w l e d g m e n t s –

Every year I teach riding clinics, training camps, seminars, and webinars to thousands of riders, trainers, auditors, and moms and dads, and each and every one of them reminds me just how incredibly lucky I am to be a coach…and how much I adore and value my career as a trainer, teacher, and mentor. I constantly remind myself to never take for granted the honor and privilege of being entrusted to share my knowledge, weird stories, and bad jokes with riders of every age, discipline, and level. From the six-year-old who wore angel wings in my jumping clinic, to the 75-year-old dressage rider who traded her walker for the mounting block, I'm eternally grateful for all the powerful gifts and experiences our incredible sport, and its amazing athletes, have blessed me with.

I'm so very grateful for the time and effort my riders, auditors, and organizers put into hosting my clinics and other educational experiences. Asking 20 (or 200) riders to stand still and pay attention can sometimes be like trying to herd cats at a dog show, but I appreciate everything everyone does to ensure my clinics are safe, empowering, educational, and enjoyable.

I'm so very grateful to the parents of young riders who allow me to be a part of their child's mental and physical development. Not just as equestrians, but as the confident, competent, and courageous young adults they're becoming. Our sport is the most wonderful classroom, and I'm humbled by the thought that I'm entrusted to be a teacher at this most amazing school.

time supporter who will remain anonymous, but who never stopped believing in my ability to become a Master in this amazing sport of ours. Your kind and generous gifts have given my words a voice and my voice a stage to speak on. The path to becoming a Master is a long and unfamiliar one, but I love that we're walking it together. While you remain behind the scenes to others, your unwavering contributions to my career and your selfless consideration toward my family will always remain front and center for me.

I am so very grateful for the many riders who agreed to share their photos in this book, but I'm even more grateful to my amazing publishing team—Caroline Robbins, Martha Cook, and Becca Didier at Trafalgar Square Books